MOZART

PIANO SONATAS K. 279–284; K. 309–311

EDITED BY STEWART GORDON

AN ALFRED MASTERWORK EDITION

Copyright © 2019 by Alfred Music
All rights reserved. Printed in USA.
ISBN-10: 1-4706-4023-6
ISBN-13: 978-1-4706-4023-1

Cover art: Afternoon Tea at the Temple *(1766)*
By Michel-Barthélémy Ollivier (French, 1712–1784)
Oil on canvas

WOLFGANG AMADEUS MOZART

Thematic Index

Piano Sonatas VOLUME I
Edited by Stewart Gordon

Contents

ABOUT THIS EDITION

Mozart scholarship and research have flourished for much of the past century. There is very little new to be uncovered about the composer's life or works. Questions remain, to be sure, with regard to precise dating of some of the composer's works, and indeed, there are unanswered questions surrounding the keyboard sonatas. Keyboard players are reminded that the composer's solo keyboard compositions represent but a small portion of Mozart's catalogue of works, and that these works, important as they are to those who perform them, are not among the most influential genres of the composer's astounding creative output.

Even so, Wolfgang Amadeus Mozart (1756–1791) grew up as a prodigious keyboard player. Written evidence supports the supposition that he performed his keyboard works regularly. Moreover, their creation was often inspired by personal relationships or circumstances. Examples are the second movement of K. 309, written as a portrait of the teenage daughter of the conductor of the Mannheim orchestra, Rose Cannabich (1764–1839), described as "sweet and charming"; the anguish of K. 310, written after the death of the composer's mother; or the impassioned energy of K. 457, written for Mozart's young student Thérèse von Trattner (1758–1793). Thus, there is every reason to revel in the assumption that the keyboard sonatas were close to the composer's heart and that studying them can lead to insight into his character and style.

The importance of improvisation and its impact on performance directions, passagework, and ornamentation leads to both challenging issues and diverse opinions as to the best way to realize the composer's intentions. Indeed, it can be safely assumed that spontaneous creativity was an important part of Mozart's own performance practice and that many details of the music might differ from performance to performance.

Sources for these sonatas are often attended by unanswered questions or uncertain speculation. Autographs in the composer's handwriting exist for only some of the sonatas, and these sometimes appear to be hastily written and may have sometimes served as the composer's skeletal guides for more elaborate or refined performances. There are often substantial differences between autographs and later publications, the latter almost always offering more elaborate details and/ or performance directions. Some scholars believe that the composer was involved in editing some of the first editions published during his lifetime and that published changes and refinements represent his wishes. Others insist there is no hard evidence that such is the case. Several of the later sonatas were published posthumously.

This edition follows the tradition of making available alternate versions of those sonatas that show substantial differences between autographs and first or early editions. The performer will be challenged to decide which version to use.

In both the autographs and first editions, double dynamic markings often appear, one marking for the right hand and another for the left hand. Some editions preserve this duplication; others compress the two markings into a single one. This edition subscribes to such compression to preserve clarity of the written page except in those cases where (1) the dynamic changes occur at different rhythmic points or (2) the passage as a whole involves a dynamic pattern suggesting both compression and the first exception. In these cases, both sets of dynamics are shown.

Phrasing from early sources has been preserved, and important differences between such sources have been noted. The differences between staccato markings, whether dots or wedges, are so sporadic and erratic in both the autographs and first editions that this text has followed the tradition of using only one type: dots.

Courtesy accidentals have been added to aid the performer—in places of the close proximity of a neighboring measure, and where the notes involved are in the same register. To preserve the clarity of the page, the courtesy accidentals are not enclosed in parentheses, and excessive courtesies have been omitted. By contrast, some passages do include accidentals that have been enclosed in parentheses; these accidentals show missing necessary accidentals that are not found in the original sources.

Like most other editors, this editor has chosen not to indicate pedal markings in the sonatas. References to pedaling in Mozart's letters indicate that the instruments he used were equipped with knee pedals. Some pianos had hand-operated devices. (*See* the following article "Mozart and the Piano.") This realization, coupled with acoustical properties of instruments of the period, renders traditional pedal markings of little help at best and misleading at worst. Performers who pedal this music on today's pianos will need to use a variety of complex pedal techniques to ensure appropriate balance and clarity, taking into account the acoustical characteristics of contemporary instruments and performance venues.

Fingering suggested throughout this edition reflects contemporary patterns that are practical on today's pianos. However, the practice of using phrase marks to indicate hand-position changes is often influential in determining suggested fingering. Playing octaves with the first and fourth fingers as a way to enhance legato is often suggested but may not be possible for some hands.

MOZART AND THE PIANO

The pianos Mozart used in the late 18th century were mostly those made in Germany and Austria. In contrasting these with pianos made in England, two early 19th-century sources used similar terms to describe the German/Austrian types. Johann Nepomuk Hummel (1778–1837) wrote that such pianos "may be played with the weakest hand," allowing the performer "every possible degree of light and shade…speaks clearly and promptly" with a "round, fluty tone."[1] Friedrich Kalkbrenner (1785–1849) described German/Austrian pianos as being "extremely easy to play," resulting in easy "precision, clarity, and rapidity of execution."[2] Typically, these instruments had

a range of five octaves, from ![bass clef note] to ![treble clef note]. They were often equipped with lever devices

activated by the knees that served to sustain the sound, the effect achieved by a foot pedal on later instruments and by the damper pedal on today's pianos.

Mozart's most extensive comments on the piano of his time are in a well-known letter to his father, written October 17–18, 1777. He had travelled to Augsburg to organize a concert and to visit the workshop of Johann Andreas Stein (1728–1792). Stein is believed to have helped Mozart with arranging details for the concert, one on which Mozart's triple piano concerto, K. 242, was performed with the composer and Stein serving as two of the soloists.

Stein had learned his piano-building trade in the Strasbourg workshop of Gottfried Silbermann (1683–1753) and later moved to Augsburg, where he built various keyboard instruments, including small organs. He was in the final stages of developing a mechanism for the piano's action, his so-called *Prellmechanik*. The device relocated the position of the hammers in the piano and provided stability for their escape away from the strings. Although he did not perfect the invention until 1781, he was able to impress Mozart with it during the composer's visit.

Mozart's letter to his father reveals not only the composer's admiration for Stein's pianos, but also his sensitivity to touch issues of the instrument itself:

> This time I shall begin at once with Stein's pianofortes. Before I had seen any of his make, Späth's claviers had always been my favourites. But now I much prefer Stein's, for they damp ever so much better than the Regensburg instruments. When I strike hard, I can keep my

---

1   Hummel, *A Complete Theoretical and Practical Course*, 64–65.
2   Kalkbrenner, *Méthode*, 8.

finger on the note or raise it, but the sound ceases the moment I have produced it. In whatever way I touch the keys, the tone is always even. It never jars, it is never stronger or weaker or entirely absent; in a word, it is always even. It is true that he does not sell a pianoforte of this kind for less than three hundred gulden, but the trouble and the labour which Stein puts into the making of it cannot be paid for. His instruments have this special advantage over others that they are made with escape action. Only one maker in a hundred bothers about this. But without an escapement it is impossible to avoid jangling and vibration after the note is struck. When you touch the keys, the hammers fall back again the moment after they have struck the strings, whether you hold down the keys or release them ... He guarantees that the sounding-board will neither break nor split. When he has finished making one for a clavier, he places it in the open air, exposing it to rain, snow, the heat of the sun and all the devils in order that it may crack. Then he inserts wedges and glues them in to make the instrument very strong and firm. He is delighted when it cracks, for he can then be sure that nothing more can happen to it. Indeed, he often cuts into it himself and then glues it together again and strengthens it in this way ... The device to which you work with your knee is better on his than on other instruments. I have only to touch it and it works; and when you shift your knee the slightest bit, you do not hear the least reverberation.[3]

Mozart's reference to Späth is the composer's only documented mention of the Regensburg piano builder Franz Jakob Späth (1714–1786). Mozart's mention of the price of Stein's instruments has generated speculation as to its being the reason the composer purchased a less costly piano built by the Viennese piano builder Gabriel Anton Walter (1752–1826). Other speculations suggest purchasing the Walter was a matter of convenience.

Born in Germany, Walter had moved to Vienna by 1780. His pianos achieved a reputation for excellence. In 1790, he was granted the title of Royal Court Chamber Organ and Instrument Maker. He produced a large number of instruments for the time, claiming in 1790 to have built 350 instruments, some of which he exported. Carl Czerny (1791–1857) mentions a Walter piano in the home of Ludwig van Beethoven when as a boy of eight he visited the composer in 1802, describing the instrument as "the best one made then."[4]

Mozart purchased the Walter sometime in 1782, and it resides currently in the composer's birthplace in Salzburg. Walter made continuing improvements to his instruments, even to those that had been purchased earlier. Thus, to what extent the instrument on display in Salzburg actually represents what the composer used has been debated. Controversy has focused especially on whether or not the instrument had knee pedals or keyboard-level hand stops when Mozart owned it, an issue that would have significant impact on performance practice.[5]

Portrait of Wolfgang Amadeus Mozart *(1789)*
By Dora Stock (German, 1760–1832)
Silverpoint

---

3   Anderson, *The Letters of Mozart and His Family*, 327–328.
4   Newman, "Beethoven's Pianos Versus His Piano Ideals," 484.
5   *See* Michael Latcham's article "Mozart and the Pianos of Gabriel Anton Walter," *Early Music*, XXV/3 (August 1997), 382–400; as well as Eva Badura-Skoda's response in "The Anton Walter Fortepiano: Mozart's Beloved Concert Instrument: A Response to Michael Latcham," *Early Music*, XXVII/3 (August 2000), 469–474.

ORNAMENTATION AND IMPROVISATION

During the period when Mozart wrote his sonatas, improvisation was an integral part of performance practice. It is likely, in fact, that Mozart's performances of his music varied from performance to performance, not only in the execution of ornamental additions such as grace notes, trills, turns, and arpeggios, but also in elaboration of melodic lines through added passagework. There is a significant amount of evidence to support this assumption. First, there are many differences between the extant autographs of sonatas and the first editions published during his lifetime. There is no conclusive evidence that the composer was involved in editing those sonatas published during his lifetime. However, he likely prepared the copy sent to the publisher from his original autograph. In doing so, he probably added more performance directions, such as articulation and dynamics, as well as more elaborate ornamentation and passagework, often in slow movements and especially in reprises. The latter frequently bear *da capo* indications in autographs, while they are written out, often with variants, in first editions.

The autograph of K. 457 discovered in 1990 is a clear example of Mozart's thinking regarding this practice. The second movement is attended by a separate page that shows fragments of the text. These present passages drawn from the movement in a more elaborate form and are notated as "variations" by the composer. It has been speculated that Mozart wrote out these "variations" to instruct the student for whom the sonata was written, Thérèse von Trattner, in the art of improvising on the original text.

During Mozart's time, the technique of improvising ornaments and passagework was, thus, a skill keyboard players were expected to develop. Performers were expected not only to be able to incorporate such a technique into their presentations, but also to display their individual sensibilities in the process. Developing such a technique is for the most part absent from present-day keyboard instruction. Current emphasis is placed, rather, on the importance of trying to recreate the music exactly as the composer wanted. Such an admirable goal generates intense study of textual details. It also, however, may lead to the expectation that there is but one correct way to execute a given ornament and the challenge is simply to find and incorporate it. Such is not the case. True, there are treatises that undertake to direct how ornaments should be realized. However, recent research has shown that, indeed, period authorities do not always agree, some suggesting or recommending different realizations of trills, turns, and grace notes.

Assessments in the early 20th century set forth the premise that the *Essay on the True Art of Playing Keyboard Instruments* of Carl Philipp Emanuel Bach (1714–1788) was the final authority for keyboard performance. His treatise was published and widely known. It was thus influential on many 18th- and early 19th-century musicians. Moreover, it is addressed specifically to keyboard players. However, recent research has pointed to the fact that other writers of the period sometimes disagreed with C. P. E. Bach. Some believe that his ornament realizations could be considered conservative, even dogmatic, when seen in the light of movement toward later performance practices, as well as the improvisational flexibility that was also an important part of the tradition.

Sandra Rosenblum points out in her exhaustive study of Classical piano music performance practices, "Although many treatises discussed ornaments and gave instructions for their performance, there was not—and is not now—complete agreement regarding either notation or performance. Since the second half of the 18th century was a time of transition, some aspects of practice can only be deduced from the musical settings of individual ornaments. Indeed, the very function of being ornamental precludes adherence to a rigorous, unambiguous system. The aesthetic basis of ornamentation requires of the performer a degree of spontaneity and nuance whose subtleties would be at best difficult, if not impossible, to notate and whose expressiveness in performance might well be lost if the notes were frozen into a rigid rhythmization."[6]

Frederick Neumann echoes Rosenblum's point of view in his 1989 study of Mozart ornamentation and improvisation: "We must not belittle the importance of historical documents on performance, but we must keep them in proper perspective; that is, we have to be aware of their unusually high degree of abstraction, aware also of the fact that ornaments lend themselves to regulation less than perhaps any other musical matter."[7] Later Neumann writes, "A transfer of rules from C. P. E. Bach to Mozart's music does not pass the test of compatibility . . . From his earliest childhood he [Mozart] absorbed the immensely rich and varied musical experiences during his foreign travels in childhood and adolescence."[8]

To examine a specific example of a frequently encountered debate: should trills start on the upper note or main note in the Mozart sonatas? The C. P. E. Bach realizations show trills starting on the upper note, a practice that had evolved as harmonic consciousness became stronger, the upper-note start providing a melodic dissonance deemed expressive.[9]

Leopold Mozart (1719–1787), Wolfgang's father, wrote *A Treatise on the Fundamental Principles of Violin Playing* in 1755. It was well known in its time and is still regarded as a significant source for period-performance practices. Although realization of ornamentation is not addressed with the same thoroughness as that of C. P. E. Bach, he agrees that the trill should begin on the upper note. The young Wolfgang may well have been influenced by his father's stance on this issue, although as Neumann has suggested, extensive travel to France and Italy as a young prodigy must have exposed Wolfgang to a variety of performance practices.

Rosenblum points out that earlier Italian performance practice often began trills on the main note, citing examples from *Il Transilvano* (1593) of Girolamo Diruta (ca. 1554–ca. 1610) and the written-out trills in the keyboard works of Girolamo Frescobaldi (1583–1643).[10] Moreover, she cites several late 18th-century sources that show starting trills on the main note: *Regole Armoniche* (1775) of Vincenzo Manfredini (1737–1799); *Principi di musica: teorico-practici* (ca. 1780) of Vincenzo Panerai (ca. 1750–ca. 1790); a table of ornaments attending a *Sonata per il clavicembalo* (ca. 1778) by Johann Abraham Peter Schulz (1747–1800); separately published realization examples for *Kuhrpfälzische Tonschule* (1778) by Abbé Georg Joseph Vogler (1749–1814); and even fingerings in an undated manuscript by Beethoven's teacher, Johann Georg Albrechtsberger (1736–1809).[11] Based on this evidence, Rosenblum concludes, "In the Classic style, the decision between a main- and an upper-note trill start may involve the balancing of factors or the relative importance given to harmonic, melodic, and sometimes rhythmic elements. The interpreter's deliberations should be guided, insofar as possible, by the style of the piece and by any known proclivities of the composer . . . [There are] numerous situations in performance practices for which the answer depends on the performer's opinion and taste."[12]

---

6   Rosenblum, *Performance Practices in Classical Piano Music*, 217.
7   Neumann, *Ornamentation and Improvisation in Mozart*, 3.
8   Ibid., 4.
9   Bach, *Essay on the True Art of Playing Keyboard Instruments*, 99–112.
10   Rosenblum, 241.
11   Ibid., 242–243.
12   Ibid., 246–247.

This flexibility may be applied to other examples of ornamentation found throughout the Mozart sonatas: grace notes (single, double, or triple), appoggiaturas, and arpeggios. It is also exemplified in current performance practice as represented by well-known performers who purport to be Mozart specialists by offering recordings of the complete sonatas, or complete piano works. Comparison of ornamental execution in these recorded performances reveals a wide variety of realizations: different start-ups and endings, speeds, and rhythmic placements.

Footnotes in this edition often reflect possible differences in realizing ornamentation, taking into account the relative importance of musical elements and performance tradition. Selected examples of footnotes inviting such considerations are K. 281, first movement footnotes ⓐ and ⓕ; K. 284, second movement footnote ⓙ; K. 310, first movement footnote ⓑ and second movement footnotes ⓐ and ⓚ; and K. 311, third movement footnote ⓗ.

This edition has attempted to provide realizations of ornaments that are within an accepted historical range of possibilities, often suggesting more than one answer. It is hoped that the performer will engage in a decision-making process that will lead to the flexibility and creativity this ever-fascinating but elusive challenge requires.

Portrait of Wolfgang Amadeus Mozart
Playing in Paris with His Father, Johann Georg Leopold,
and His Sister, Maria Anna *(1763)*
By Louis Carrogis Carmontelle (French, 1717–1806)
Watercolor on paper

SOURCES AND EARLY EDITIONS

Sonata(s)	Date of Composition	Autograph(s)	First and/or Early Edition(s) (Multiple editions are listed in chronological order.)
K. 279–283	ca. 1774	Extant except for the first movement of K. 279 (Biblioteka Jagiellońska, Kraków, Poland)	Breitkopf & Härtel: *Complete Works*, Leipzig, 1799 Johann Anton André: Offenbach am Main, *Selected Sonatas*, 1841
K. 284	ca. 1774	Extant (Biblioteka Jagiellońska, Kraków, Poland)	Christoph Torricella: with K. 333, Vienna, 1784
K. 309	1777	Autograph believed to be in the handwriting of Leopold Mozart (ca. 1788) (private collection)	Franz Joseph Heina: with K. 310 and K. 311, Paris, ca. 1778–1782
K. 310	1778	Extant (Morgan Library and Museum, New York, New York)	Heina: *see* K. 309 above.
K. 311	1777	Extant (Biblioteka Jagiellońska, Kraków, Poland)	Heina: *see* K. 309 above.
K. 330	ca. 1880	Extant (Biblioteka Jagiellońska, Kraków, Poland)	Artaria: with K. 331 and K. 332, Vienna, 1784
K. 331	ca. 1880	Only part of the third movement: m. 90 to the end (private collection)	Artaria: *see* K. 330 above. Breitkopf & Härtel: *Complete Works*, Leipzig, 1841
K. 332	ca. 1880	Extant except for part of the last movement: m. 107 to the end (William H. Scheide Collection, Princeton University Library, New Jersey)	Artaria: *see* K. 330 above.
K. 333	1783	Extant (Berlin State Library)	Christoph Torricella: with K. 284, Vienna, 1784
K. 457	1784	Extant: copyist's autograph with corrections in the composer's handwriting (Jewish National and University Library, Jerusalem); composer's autograph discovered in 1990 in Philadelphia (now in Internationale Stiftung Mozarteum, Biblioteca Mozartiana)	Artaria: with the Fantasia K. 475, Vienna, 1785 Johann Anton André: with the Fantasia K. 475, 1802
K. 475 (Fantasia)	1785	Extant: discovered in 1990 in Philadelphia (now in Internationale Stiftung Mozarteum, Biblioteca Mozartiana)	*See* K. 457 above.
K. 533	1788	None, but an unrevised autograph of K. 494, a rondo published in 1786 revised and used for the third movement of this work, is extant (private collection)	Franz Anton Hoffmeister: Vienna, 1788
K. 545	1788	None	Bureau d'Arts et d'Industrie: Vienna, 1805
K. 570	1789	Fragment of first movement: mm. 65–132 and 161 to the end (British Library, London)	Artaria: Vienna, 1796
K. 576	1789	None	Bureau d'Arts et d'Industrie: Vienna, 1805 Johann Anton André: Offenbach am Main, 1805

SELECTED RECORDINGS OF THE COMPLETE MOZART PIANO SONATAS

Artist	Record Label	Year
Arrau, Claudio	Philips Records	1991 (remastered)
Barenboim, Daniel	EMI Classics	1991
Biegel, Jeffrey	Entertainment One Music (eOne Music)	2009 (Vol. 1), 2015 (Vol. 2)
Brautigam, Ronald	Bis	2000
De Larrocha, Alicia	RCA	2003
Endres, Michael	Ohms Classics	2004
Entremont, Philippe	Pro Arte	1990
Eschenbach, Christoph	Deutsche Grammophon	1999
Gieseking, Walter	EMI Classics	1951–1955 (rereleased by Profil/Hänssler, 2018)
Gould, Glenn	Columbia Masterworks	1968–1975 (rereleased by Sony Classical, 1994)
Gulda, Friedrich	Deutsche Grammophon	2009 (posthumous release)
Haebler, Ingrid	Denon	1990s (remastered on Phillips)
Jandó, Jenő	Naxos	1991
Klien, Walter	Vox	2007
Kraus, Lili	Sony	1967–1968
Mauser, Siegfried	Celestial Harmonies	2014
Pires, Maria João	Deutsche Grammophon	2006
Say, Fazıl	Warner Classics	2016
Schiff, András	London Records	1995
Uchida, Mitsuko	Decca	2003
van Oort, Bart	Brilliant Classics	2012
Würtz, Klára	Brilliant Classics	1998

TEMPOS IN MOZART'S PIANO SONATAS

When Mozart visited Augsburg in 1777, he forged a friendship with the piano builder Johann Andreas Stein. During the visit, Mozart was asked to hear Stein's eight-year-old daughter, Maria Anna (1769–1833), who was celebrated locally as a child prodigy. Mozart wrote of the encounter to his father on October 24, severely criticizing the technique of the young pianist and stating, "Further, she will never acquire the most essential, the most difficult and chief requisite in music, which is, time, because from her earlier years she has done her utmost not to play in time." Later in the letter, Mozart comments, "Everyone is amazed that I can always keep strict time. What these people cannot grasp is that tempo rubato in an Adagio, the left hand should go on playing in strict time."[13]

This comment, coupled with Mozart's frequent use of qualifying terms attached to typical period indications (*allegro, adagio, andante,* etc.), points to the composer's sensitivity to both tempo indications and expressive content. In the piano sonatas, there are many instances of such qualifying terms. Some examples are *Allegro con spirito* (K. 309 and 311, first movements); *Allegro assai* (K. 332, third movement); *Allegro moderato* (K. 330, first movement); *Andante un poco adagio* (K. 309, second movement); and *Allegretto grazioso* (K. 333, third movement).

Mozart's tempo indications predate the metronome. Johann Nepomuk Maelzel (1772–1838) did not begin manufacturing metronomes in Paris until 1816, after having appropriated the mechanism from a Netherlands inventor, Dietrich Nikolaus Winkel (1777–1826). Thus, in Mozart's time there was no concept of using a numerical scale to regulate tempo, much less attaching traditional terms such as *Allegro* or *Andante* to such a scale. Moreover, the relationship between the metric time signature and its attending tempo indication was a flexible one with other factors entering into the tempo determination, such as the character of the music, the smallest note value, articulation, and accentuation.

As a result of these historical circumstances, Mozart's tempo indications have been a constant subject for research and speculation. Ongoing analysis is represented by two recent works: *The Tempo Indications of Mozart* by Jean-Pierre Marty and *Mozarts Tempo System: Ein Handbuch für die professionelle Praxis* by Helmut Breidenstein. (*See* "Sources Consulted.")

Performers considered to be Mozart specialists conceive movements at different tempos, sometimes with minimal differences, but sometimes with differences substantial enough to influence the overall effect of the movement. The tempos of five such performers are recorded in the following table. Reducing to a metronomic number the pulse flexibility evidenced in broadened cadential points, shaped phrases, or reflected in the changing moods of different sections is often elusive. Even so, the table serves the purpose of representing the differences that attend these artists' challenge in finding the "right" tempo. From among the many performers who have devoted their efforts to recording the complete sonatas of Mozart, the five chosen for this representation are Daniel Barenboim (1942–), Walter Gieseking (1895–1956), Ingrid Haebler (1926–), András Schiff (1953–), and Mitsuko Uchida (1948–).

---

13 Anderson, *The Letters of Mozart and His Family*, 340.

Sonata	Tempo and Time Signature	Rhythmic Unit	Barenboim	Gieseking	Haebler	Schiff	Uchida
K. 279	Allegro 𝄴	♩ =	130	118	108	114	125
	Andante 3/4	♩ =	62–64	57–58	60–62	68–70	70–72
	Allegro 2/4	♩ =	148	152	122–124	139	138
K. 280	Allegro assai 3/4	♩ =	140–142	140	132–136	136–138	142–144
	Adagio 6/8	♪ =	78–80	108–110	98–100	106–108	76–80
	Presto 3/8	♩. =	108–112	98	96–98	102	108–112
K. 281	Allegro 2/4	♩ =	76–78	70–72	64	73–75	72–74
	Andante amoroso 3/8	♪ =	90–94	88–90	100–102	94–96	104–108
	Rondeau: Allegro 𝄵	𝅗𝅥 =	98–100	78	80–82	100–102	83–84
K. 282	Adagio 𝄴	♩ =	40–42	42–44	40–42	46–47	44–46
	Menuetto I 3/4	♩ =	138	142	126	122	132
	Menuetto II 3/4	♩ =	142	138	120	116	130
	Allegro 2/4	♩ =	136	142	126	140	126–128
K. 283	Allegro 3/4	♩ =	134–138	136–138	128–130	138–140	148–150
	Andante 𝄴	♩ =	58	40	45–46	63	52
	Presto 3/8	♩. =	110–112	108	90–92	104	102
K. 284	Allegro 𝄴	♩ =	147	140	126–128	150–152	150
	Rondeau en Polonaise: Andante 3/4	♩ =	64–66	80	60–64	82–84	80
	Thema: Andante 𝄵	𝅗𝅥 =	74	76–78	70–72	75–84	74
	Variation XI: Adagio cantabile 𝄵	♩ =	40–42	44–46	42–44	55–56	46–48
	Variation XII: Allegro 3/4	♩ =	142	159	130–132	150–152	146–148
K. 309	Allegro con spirito 𝄴	𝅗𝅥 =	82	82	73	84	82
	Andante un poco adagio 3/4	♩ =	42–44	40–42	42–44	44–46	58–60
	Rondeau: Allegretto grazioso 2/4	♩ =	94	85–87	75	80–83	92
K. 310	Allegro maestoso 𝄴	♩ =	132	126–128	122	136–138	136–138
	Andante cantabile 3/4	♩ =	38	38–40	42	38	42–44
	Presto 2/4	𝅗𝅥 =	105–108	102	96–98	102	108–112
K. 311	Allegro con spirito 𝄴	♩ =	150	136	132	144–146	144
	Andante con espressione 2/4	♩ =	75	79	80–84	86–88	96
	Rondeau: Allegro 6/8	♩. =	104	102	90–92	94–98	108

SOURCES CONSULTED

Bibliography:

Anderson, Emily, ed. *The Letters of Mozart and His Family*. 3rd ed. London: Macmillan, 1989.

Bach, Carl Philipp Emanuel. *Essay on the True Art of Playing Keyboard Instruments*. Translated and edited by William J. Mitchell. New York: W. W. Norton, 1949.

Badura-Skoda, Eva. "The Anton Walter Fortepiano: Mozart's Beloved Concert Instrument: A Response to Michael Latcham." *Early Music*, XXVII/3 (August 2000), 469–474.

Badura-Skoda, Eva and Paul Badura-Skoda. *Interpreting Mozart on the Keyboard*. Translated by Leo Black. London: Barrie and Rockliff, 1962.

Breidenstein, Helmut. *Mozarts Tempo System: Ein Handbuch für die Professionelle Praxis* (Mozart's Tempo System: A Handbook for Professional Practice). Tutzing: Hans Schneider Verlag, 2011. An English translation by Lindsay Chalmers-Gerbracht and the author is available online at http://www.academia.edu/5830870/Mozarts_Tempo-System

Hummel, Johann Nepomuk. *A Complete Theoretical and Practical Course of Instructions on the Art of Playing the Piano Forte: Commencing with the Simplest Elementary Principles and Including Every Information Requisite to the Most Finished Style of Performance*. London: Boosey and Co., 1829.

Igrec, Srebrenka. "Béla Bartók's Edition of Mozart's Piano Sonatas." (1993.) *LSU Historical Dissertations and Theses*. 5644. https://digitalcommons.lsu.edu/gradschool_disstheses/5644

Irving, John. *Mozart's Piano Sonatas: Contexts, Sources, Style*. Cambridge: Cambridge University Press, 1997.

Kalkbrenner, Friederich. *Méthode pour apprendre le piano-forte a l'aide du guide-mains* (Opus 108). Paris: J. Meissonier fils, 1831. Translated by Alex Robertson. Edinburgh: Alex Robertson, n.d.

Kinderman, William. *Mozart's Piano Music*. New York: Oxford Univeristy Press, 2006.

Landon, H. C. Robbins, ed. *The Mozart Compendium*. London: Thames and Hudson, Ltd., 1990.

Latcham, Michael. "Mozart and the Pianos of Gabriel Anton Walter." *Early Music*, XXV/3 (August 1997), 382–400.

Marty, Jean-Pierre. *The Tempo Indications of Mozart*. New Haven: Yale University Press, 1989.

Mozart, Leopold. *Versuch einer gründlichen Violinschule* (A Treatise on the Fundamental Principles of Violin Playing) (1756). Translated by Editha Knocker (1948). 2nd ed. reprint. New York: Oxford University Press, 1985.

Neumann, Frederick. *Ornamentation and Improvisation in Mozart*. Princeton: Princeton University Press, 1986.

Neumann, H. and C. Schacter. "The Two Versions of Mozart's Rondo, K. 494." W. J. Mitchell and F. Salzer eds. *The Music Forum I*, 1967, 1–34.

Newman, William S. "Beethoven's Pianos Versus His Piano Ideals." *Journal of the American Musicological Society*, XXIII/3 (Fall 1970), 484–504.

Plath, Wolfgang. "Zur Datierung der Klaviersonaten KV 279–284," *Acta Mozartiana*, XXI (1974), 26–30.

Rosenblum, Sandra P. *Performance Practices in Classic Piano Music*. Bloomington: Indiana University Press, 1991.

Schlager, Karl-Heinz. *Wolfgang Amadeus Mozart: Verzeichnis von Erst- und Frühdrucken bis etwa 1800* (Wolfgang Amadeus Mozart: List of First and Early Editions to About 1800). Kassel: Bärenreiter-Verlag, 1978.

Sumner, William Leslie. *The Pianoforte*. London: MacDonald and Co., 1966.

Tyson, Alan. *Mozart: Studies of the Autograph Scores*. Cambridge: Harvard University Press, 1987.

Editions:

Numerous editions of the keyboard sonatas have appeared throughout the 19th and 20th centuries. The selected list that follows is based on editions still encountered, publishers continuing to make them available. Earlier publications often show significant editorial revisions in accordance with the practice of the time. Late 20th-century editions are much less likely to show editorial revisions of early sources.

Mozart, Wolfgang Amadeus. *Klaviersonaten*. 2 vols. Edited by Ernst Herttrich. Fingering by Hans-Martin Theopold. Munich: Henle Verlag, 1992.

———. *Klaviersonaten*. 2 vols. Edited by Ulrich Leisinger. Fingering by Heinz Scholz. Notes on interpretation by Robert D. Levin. Vienna: Wiener Urtext Edition, Schott/Universal Edition, 2003.

———. *Nineteen Sonatas for the Piano*. Edited by Julius Epstein. New York: G. Schirmer, 1893.

———. *Nineteen Sonatas for the Piano*. Edited by Sigmund Lebert and William Scharfenberg. New York: G. Schirmer, 1893.

———. *Oeuvres complètes pour piano seul*. Vols. 1 and 2: *Sonatas*. Edited by Camille Saint-Saëns. Paris: Durand et Fils, 1915.

———. *Oeuvres complèttes de Wolfgang Amadeus Mozart*. Cahier I. Leipzig: Breitkopf & Härtel, 1798.

———. *Piano Sonatas*. 2 vols. Edited by Wolfgang Plath and Wolfgang Rehm. Kassel: Bärenreiter Verlag, 1986.

———. *Sonatas and Fantasies for the Piano*. Edited by Nathan Broder. King of Prussia, PA: Theodore Presser Company, 1956.

———. *Sonatas for Pianoforte*. 2 vols. Edited by Stanley Sadie and Denis Matthews. London: Associated Board of the Royal Schools of Music, 1970–1981.

———. *Sonatas*. 2 vols. Edited by Carl Adolf Martienssen and Wilhelm Weismann. Frankfurt: Edition Peters, 1985.

———. *Sonaten und Phantasien für das Pianoforte*. Vol. 20 of *Wolfgang Amadeus Mozarts Werke*, edited by Otto Goldschmidt, Joseph Joachim, Carl Reinecke, Ernst Rudorff, and Paul Waldersee. Leipzig: Breitkopf und Härtel, 1878.

———. *Twenty Sonatas*. Edited by Béla Bartók. 1910–1912. Preface and translation by Alexander Lipsky. Kalmus edition. Reprint of first edition, Van Nuys: Alfred Music, 1985.

ACKNOWLEDGMENTS

The editor wishes to acknowledge the invaluable assistance of Albert Mendoza in the preparation of this edition. His intelligent musicianship and extraordinary editorial skills were a vital contribution to every phase of its production. Many thanks go to Bruce Nelson for his expert engraving work and his years of dedication to this publication, and to Tom Gerou and Junko Tamura for their contributions.

According to the Köchel listing, the set of sonatas K. 279–284 (later revised as numbers 189d–h and 205b) were composed in 1777. More recent research by Wolfgang Plath (1930–1995) suggests an earlier period, perhaps late 1774 or 1775, the claim partially supported by the watermarks on paper purchased around that time and partially by a letter dated December 21, 1774, from Leopold Mozart to his wife, directing "Nannerl"—Wolfgang's older sister, Maria Anna (1751–1829)—to take Wolfgang's sonatas with her as she undertook upcoming travel from Salzburg to Munich.[14] Presumably these sonatas were the ones referenced in the letter, for no other piano sonatas from this period in the composer's life have been identified.[15] Wolfgang was in Munich at the time overseeing the production of his opera *La finta giardiniera*. He performed these six sonatas several times over the next months, claiming to have played them often from memory in Munich and Augsburg, and later in Mannheim.[16]

Autographs are extant as sources for all of the set except the first movement of K. 279. These are deemed to be working autographs, quite possibly representing the first writing down of music the composer had conceived earlier and probably played in improvised versions.[17] This edition has used the autographs as the primary source when discrepancies exist between them and later editions. Since the autograph of the first movement of K. 279 is missing, two editions have become important as sources: the first edition published by Breitkopf & Härtel in 1799, as well as a later edition published by Johann Anton André (1775–1842) in 1841.

Later editions of these sonatas show many discrepancies, with the autographs as well as among the various editions themselves. Significant differences are noted in footnotes. In many cases, dynamics, articulation, use of arpeggios, and other small details appear only once and are omitted in passages where similar directions would seem appropriate, such as between expositions and recapitulations in sonata-allegro movements. These directions are often added in parentheses.

The autograph of K. 284 is often scrutinized because it shows a crossed-out version of the first movement, up to the middle of the development section (about 60 measures). This rejected start is then followed by the current version. The sonata was written for Baron Thaddeus Wolfgang von Dürnitz (1756–1807), who is described in writings of the time as an amateur pianist and bassoonist and who wrote several sonatas for bassoon and piano. The K. 284 sonata was published in Vienna by Christoph Torricella (1715–1798) in 1784, almost a decade after its composition. It was combined with K. 333 and the sonata for violin and piano K. 454, the three works designated as Op. VII.

The published version of K. 284 exhibits a significant number of changes from the earlier autograph: some text revisions, added dynamic markings, and more detailed or changed articulation. Some scholars have suggested that these revisions were made by Mozart in preparation for publication and represent the composer's thoughts about his music at a more mature stage of his career. Others have questioned this assumption. This editor has attempted to forge a middle ground. Performance details from the Torricella first edition, such as dynamic markings and articulation, are shown in parentheses. Actual text revisions have been noted in more detail, so that the performer may decide which version to choose. If, indeed, the published version represents the composer's later thinking about the work, comparing the two versions becomes a useful study of his evolving musical thought processes and improvisational creativity.

---

14 Plath, "Zur Datierung der Klaviersonaten KV 279–284," 26–30.
15 Anderson, *The Letters of Mozart and His Family*, 252–253.
16 Ibid., 328.
17 For a fascinating theory on the composer's writing procedure, *see* John Irving, *Mozart's Piano Sonatas: Context, Sources, Style*, 57–61.

SONATA IN C MAJOR, K. 279

Key: C major
Tempo: **Allegro**
Time signature: **C**
Form: sonata-allegro (with sections repeated)

Section	Measures	Analysis
Exposition	1–16	The *first theme* begins with opening chords and passagework (1–5), followed by short, lyrical phrases interspersed with broken chords in 16th notes (5–14), and a rising group of 16th notes with short trills (14–16).
	16–20	A *transition* follows of LH broken chords and RH scales, emphasizing V/ii and V/I in G major (the dominant).
	20–31	The *second theme* consists of G major motives and scales, decorated with grace notes and trills.
	31–38	The *closing section* G major figuration is based on broken chords and scales, ending with decorated rising figures.
Development	39–57	Opening in G minor, the *first theme* is referenced and extended (39–47 and 51–55), interrupted briefly by material seemingly derived from the short, lyrical phrases of the *first theme* (48–51).
Recapitulation	58–100	All material from the *exposition* is repeated with small variations, the *second theme* area staying in the home key of C major.

Key: F major
Tempo: **Andante**
Time signature: $\frac{3}{4}$
Form: sonata-allegro (with sections repeated)

Section	Measures	Analysis
Exposition	1–10	The *first theme* opens with RH lyrical fragments above triplet figuration in the LH, followed by triplets in both hands. Triplets occur throughout the movement.
	11–28	In the *second theme*, the triplets continue, often shared by both hands, in the dominant key (C major).
Development	28–42	The *first theme* is stated in C major and then passes through G minor and D minor.
Recapitulation	43–74	All material from the *exposition* is repeated with small variations, the *second theme* area staying in the home key of F major and the closing extended slightly.

Key: C major
Tempo: **Allegro**
Time signature: $\frac{2}{4}$
Form: sonata-allegro (with sections repeated)

Section	Measures	Analysis
Exposition	1–22	The *first theme* presents RH half notes that alternate with 16th-note passagework (1–10). Modulation toward the dominant occurs in 16th-note passagework (11–22).
	22–56	The *second theme* area in the dominant (G major) opens with a motive of repeated notes and two-note slurs (22–32), followed by a short transition (34–38), and then a section of staccato RH eighth notes, punctuated with rests and attended by grace notes (38–46). A *closing section* (46–56) consists of 16th notes and unresolved cadences, until the end.
Development	56–76	The repeated-note portion of the *second theme* opens, and its fragments move through several keys.
	76–86	The *first theme* is stated in E minor, passes through D minor, and then sets up a return to the tonic.
Recapitulation	86–158	All material from the *exposition* is repeated with small variations, the *second theme* area staying in the home key of C major (108–134). The *second theme* is extended to serve as a *coda* (135–158).

SONATA IN F MAJOR, K. 280

1st Movement

Key: F major
Tempo: **Allegro assai**
Time signature: ¾
Form: sonata-allegro (with sections repeated)

Section	Measures	Analysis
Exposition	1–26	The *first theme* opens with an arpeggiated chord followed by melodic fragments (1–12). Then, RH triplets punctuated by LH octaves move through chromatic harmonies to set up the dominant key (13–26).
	27–56	The *second theme* area in C major consists of a LH octave motive answered by RH 16th notes (27–34), a return of the previously introduced triplet texture (35–42), and a *closing section* that features 16th-note passagework divided between the hands (43–56).
Development	57–82	Triplets in the LH are answered by a dotted rhythm (♪.♪♪.♪) in the RH (57–66). The *second theme* passes through D minor, G minor, C major, and F major (67–74), and then is followed by *transition* material (75–82).
Recapitulation	83–144	All material presented in the *exposition* is repeated with small variations. The *second theme* area in the home key (F major) is extended by six measures (117–122).

2nd Movement

Key: F minor
Tempo: **Adagio**
Time signature: 6/8
Form: sonata-allegro (with sections repeated)

Section	Measures	Analysis
Exposition	1–8	The *first theme* opens with a short RH trill and presents a lyrical melody in a siciliano-like dotted rhythm.
	9–24	The *second theme* in A-flat major, beginning after a fermata, consists of LH broken-chord patterns supporting RH fragments interspersed with rests (9–18). A *closing section* features the return of the *first theme* dotted rhythm fragment (21–24).
Development	25–36	The *first theme* opens the *development* with diminished-7th harmony (25–28) and is extended with imitative fragments in three voice levels (29–32). The *first theme* is then stated in C minor (33–36).
Recapitulation	37–60	All material presented in the *exposition* is repeated with small variations, the *second theme* slightly extended and in the home key (F minor).

3rd Movement

Key: F major
Tempo: **Presto**
Time signature: 3/8
Form: sonata-allegro (with sections repeated)

Section	Measures	Analysis
Exposition	1–37	The *first theme* is playful, featuring eighth notes attended by a grace notes followed by rests and 16th-note passagework (1–16). Then, double 6ths and 3rds are followed by RH broken chords and two-note phrases interspersed with rests (17–37).
	38–77	The *second theme* area begins after a fermata and is in the key of C major. A dotted rhythm (♪.♪♪), sometimes attended by double grace notes, permeates; it first occurs in the RH and then in both hands (38–53). Then, RH 16th-note figuration closes the section, interrupted briefly by eighth notes and rests (54–77).
Development	78–106	The *second theme* opens in C minor and then is repeated in B-flat minor, each statement followed by phrases supported by rapid broken octaves (78–97). Short 16th-note phrases lead to a climactic half cadence in D minor followed by rests (98–107).
Recapitulation	107–190	All material presented in the *exposition* is repeated, the *second theme* area in the home key (F major).

SONATA IN B-FLAT MAJOR, K. 281

Key: B-flat major
Tempo: **Allegro**
Time signature: $\frac{2}{4}$
Form: sonata-allegro (with sections repeated)

Section	Measures	Analysis
Exposition	1–17	In the *first theme*, a trill is followed by triplet 16th notes, arpeggiated chords, and 32nd notes. Then, a repeated-note LH accompaniment supports RH scalar passagework.
	17–40	The *second theme* area in F major features florid 32nd-note passagework (22–26), 16th-note melodic fragments (27–33), and a *closing section* (34–40).
Development	41–69	The *development* opens with a melody derived from a *second theme* fragment (41–44). A reference to the *first theme* (45–48) is followed by a passage of 16th-note triplets and another of 32nd notes juxtaposed with lyrical fragments, touching on G minor, C minor, and E-flat major (48–69).
Recapitulation	70–109	The material presented in the *exposition* is repeated, the *second theme* area remaining in the home key (B-flat major).

Key: E-flat major
Tempo: **Andante amoroso**
Time signature: $\frac{3}{8}$
Form: sonata-allegro (with sections repeated)

Section	Measures	Analysis
Exposition	1–15	The *first theme* opens with wide-ranging descending scales followed by 16th-note scale fragments and triplet 16th-note broken chords.
	16–28	A transitional melody is accompanied by LH broken-chord patterns and modulates to the dominant key (B-flat major).
	28–46	The *second theme* opens with triplet 16th notes played by both hands a 10th apart (28–31). The triplets become the LH accompaniment for long, lyrical RH melodies (32–42). A short *closing section* returns to RH 16th-note triplets (43–46).
Development	47–58	RH and LH 16th-note triplets, as well as lyrical fragments, are derived from the *second theme*.
Recapitulation	59–106	The *first theme* is varied with the addition of 16th-note triplets in both hands. A surprising inverted dominant harmony is introduced (61–63), allowing the transitional melody to open in A-flat major and modulate to the home key (E-flat major) (74–88). The *second theme* material then unfolds in the home key without variation.

Key: B-flat major
Tempo: **Rondeau – Allegro**
Time signature: ¢
Form: rondo – **ABACADABA** (the C section in two-part form, each part repeated)

Section	Measures	Analysis
A	1–27	An *opening theme* features slurred two-note patterns (1–8), followed by triplet passagework (8–17). A *transition* passage continues the eighth-note triplets, first as a LH accompaniment and then shared with both hands (18–27).
B	28–43	A *new theme* is presented in F major, the triplets continuing both as accompaniment and melody (28–39). The RH trills of the following passage lead to a fermata and a free, cadenza-like extension of m. 43 (39–43).
A	43–51	Eight measures of the **A** theme are presented.
C	52–71	An *eight-measure theme*, marked to be repeated, opens in G minor and closes in the dominant (D major) (52–59). A second *eight-measure segment* opens in the dominant and resolves to G minor (60–67). Three measures of *transition* (68–70) set up the home key (B-flat major).
A	71–89	The first 16 measures of the *opening theme* are stated, followed by the introduction of the note A-flat to set up the key of E-flat major.
D	90–114	A *12-measure lyrical theme* unfolds in E-flat major (90–101). A *transition* re-introduces eighth-note triplets and sets up the home key (B-flat major) (102–114).
A	114–123	The eight-measure fragment of the *opening theme* is varied with extended, cadenza-like trills, first in the RH and then the LH.
B	124–142	The **B** theme is presented completely in the home key (B-flat major).
A	142–162	The first portion of the **A** theme is presented as it originally appeared but is extended slightly to close the work.

SONATA IN E-FLAT MAJOR, K. 282

Key: E-flat major
Tempo: **Adagio**
Time signature: **C**
Form: two-part form (each part repeated), coda

Section	Measures	Analysis
A	1–8	The *first theme* begins with a stately opening melody in eighth and 16th notes, modulating to a half cadence in the dominant key (B-flat major). At m. 4, the LH harmonic support consists of 16th-note broken chords.
	9–15	A *second theme* comprised of 16th and 32nd notes is stated in B-flat major. The end of the section is marked with a repeat.
B	16–26	The *opening theme* material is stated with different harmony, much like a development section (16–21). The LH 16th-note broken chords return at m. 22, supporting melodic fragments reminiscent of the melody presented in mm. 4–8.
	27–33	The material presented in mm. 9–15 is repeated in the home key (E-flat major). Repeat signs indicate a return to m. 16.
Coda	34–36	Three measures present a varied version of the opening phrase of the movement and cadence in the home key.

Key: B-flat major
Tempo: **Menuetto I and II**
Time signature: **¾**
Form: **AB CD** (with each part repeated), *da capo* **AB**

Section	Measures	Analysis
A	1–12	Upbeats attend statements of the *main theme* of *Menuetto I*, which consists of eighth and quarter notes. The section ends in the dominant key (F major) and is marked to be repeated.
B	12–32	Opening with a series of chromatically descending chords, the **B** section paraphrases material from the **A** section. It closes in the home key (B-flat major) and is marked to be repeated.
C	32–48	Opening in E-flat major, the theme that begins *Menuetto II* sounds somewhat similar to those of the **A** section, using 16th notes, dotted rhythms, and eighth-note triplets. It cadences in the dominant (B-flat major) and is marked to be repeated.
D	48–72	The first eight measures of the **D** section represent a short departure from the theme presented in **C**. At the upbeat to m. 57, the **C** theme is repeated and slightly extended. It cadences in the tonic (E-flat major), and the section is marked to be repeated. An indication of *Menuetto I da capo* directs the performer to return to play sections **A** and **B**, without repeats.

Key: E-flat major
Tempo: **Allegro**
Time signature: **2/4**
Form: sonata-allegro (with sections repeated)

Section	Measures	Analysis
Exposition	1–8	An unusually short *first theme* ends on a half cadence, setting up the dominant key (B-flat major).
	8–39	Three ideas make up the *second theme* area: an opening idea with dotted rhythms and RH trills (8–19); RH chords with arpeggio indications, followed by 16th notes and RH syncopation (20–30); and a *closing section* of RH 16th-note passagework (31–39).
Development	39–62	The *first theme* is stated and fragmented, passing through several keys, including B-flat minor, E-flat minor, and C minor.
Recapitulation	62–102	The material presented in the *exposition* is repeated. The *second theme* area remains in the tonic (E-flat major), and the *closing section* is slightly extended.

SONATA IN G MAJOR, K. 283

1st Movement 75

Key: G major
Tempo: **Allegro**
Time signature: ¾
Form: sonata-allegro (with sections repeated)

Section	Measures	Analysis
Exposition	1–22	The *first theme* consists of two segments: the first features two-note phrases in the RH interrupted by 16th-note scales and broken triads (1–16); the second consists of a series of RH broken 3rds supported by LH octaves and ends with a short trill (16–22).
	23–53	The *second theme* area is in the dominant (D major) and opens with a syncopated lyrical line that is repeated and varied (23–31). Passages of two-note slurs and 16th-note passagework follow (31–43). Then, a *closing section* brings back the RH broken 3rds, this time with added trills, as well as briefly the syncopated lyrical line (43–53).
Development	54–71	*Exposition* material is not directly developed. Instead, a short *new theme* appears in D major (54–62), followed by descending double notes in the RH, over a LH pedal point on the note D, and a short *transition* (62–71).
Recapitulation	71–120	The material presented in the *exposition* is repeated, the *second theme* area remaining in the home key (G major).

2nd Movement 80

Key: C major
Tempo: **Andante**
Time signature: ¢
Form: sonata-allegro (with sections repeated, attended by first and second endings)

Section	Measures	Analysis
Exposition	1–4	A *first theme* consists of an opening repeated-note phrase and its answer.
	5–6	A *transition* features RH dotted rhythm and modulates to G major.
	7–15	The *second theme* area presents RH scale-like passages in 16th notes (7–10), then four measures of a lyrical, ornamented *closing theme*. The first ending at m. 14 leads back to C major, and the second ending at m. 15 leads to diminished-7th figuration that opens the *development* section.
Development	16–24	The LH and RH imitate each other in outlining a diminished-7th figure that leads to a statement of the *first theme* in D minor (15–18). A repetition of the *first theme* leads to A minor, as the slurred interval of a diminished 5th that ends the first phrase is inverted and extended (19–24).
Recapitulation	25–41	The material from the *exposition* is presented with an interesting change: the *opening theme* unexpectedly modulates to F major in m. 28 and moves to its dominant for the *second theme* area (C major, the home key) in mm. 28–30. The *second theme* area then unfolds in the home key as expected. The first ending leads back to the diminished-7th opening of the *development* section, and the second ending closes the movement in the home key.

3rd Movement 84

Key: G major
Tempo: **Presto**
Time signature: ⅜
Form: sonata-allegro (with sections repeated), coda

Section	Measures	Analysis
Exposition	1–40	The *first theme* opens with an energetic RH melody over LH repeated notes, 16th-note passagework in each hand, and a syncopated descending line (1–24). A *transition* follows, continuing with measure-long chords, 16th notes in each hand, and short phrases that recall the opening, before modulating to the dominant (D major) (25–40).
	41–102	The *second theme* area opens with a phrase of three eighth notes presented sequentially and then contrapuntally, passing between the hands (41–64). A *closing section* alters the three-note motive and contrasts it with broken chords, RH tremolos, and a chromatic line of staccato eighth notes in both hands, closing the section in D major (73–102).
Development	103–171	A short fragment opens in D minor and moves to A minor through broken RH chords in 16th notes. These move to E minor, extending the broken arpeggios with figural pedal points, first in the LH and then the RH (103–138). Then, the chromatic line of staccato eighth notes leads to contrasting *forte* and *piano* chords, imitative phrases passed between the hands, and a final rising chromatic scale in the RH that sets up the return to the home key (G major) (138–171).
Recapitulation	172–277	The material presented in the *exposition* is repeated, the *second theme* area remaining in the home key (G major). A final authentic cadence of four measures is designated *coda*.

SONATA IN D MAJOR, K. 284

1st Movement 90

Key: D major
Tempo: **Allegro**
Time signature: **c**
Form: sonata-allegro (with sections repeated)

Section	Measures	Analysis
Exposition	1–12	The *first theme* opens with an arpeggiated tonic chord and a monophonic line in both hands, followed by melodic fragments in double notes and 16th notes.
	12–21	A *transition* opens with a RH orchestral tremolo in 16th notes (13–17). Then, the 16th notes become LH figuration below RH eighth-note melodic fragments (17–21). The *transition* ends by modulating to the dominant key (A major).
	22–51	The *second theme* area opens with an eight-measure melody (22–29), followed by an extended section of display passages featuring RH tremolos and melodic figures (29–37). Broken-chord RH passagework is punctuated with LH octaves and a rhythmic chordal cadence (38–45). A *closing section* features a measure-long RH trill (46–51).
Development	52–71	Material from the *exposition* is not quoted literally, but melodic fragments may be derived from earlier material: mm. 52–59 from 17–20, and 61–65 from 9–12. The melodic fragments are often played by the LH with frequent crosses over the RH, a showy virtuosic gesture of the period. The display is accompanied by 16th-note passagework.
Recapitulation	72–127	The material presented in the *exposition* is repeated, the *second theme* area remaining in the home key (D major) and the *closing section* extended (118–127).

2nd Movement 97

Key: A major
Tempo: **Rondeau en Polonaise – Andante**
Time signature: **3/4**
Form: rondo – **ABACBA** coda

Section	Measures	Analysis
A	1–16	The first eight measures are repeated with figural variations in the melody. A distinctive characteristic of the *main theme* is that *forte* motives are answered immediately by *piano* fragments.
B	17–30	The **B** section opens in A major and modulates to the dominant (E major). A scalar line is decorated with ornaments (17–20). Then, two measures (21 and 22) contain the rhythmic figure (♪♩.) known as *Lombard rhythm* or the *Scotch snap*, again with *forte-piano* contrasts. The section closes with scale-like passagework in the RH, still marked with the aforementioned dynamic contrasts (25–30).
A	31–46	The *main theme* is stated and repeated, varied from its first presentation by sometimes reversing the *forte-piano* dynamic contrasts and by changing the final cadence to set up the new key of the next section.
C	47–52	A theme in F-sharp minor features RH repeated notes and trills.
B	53–69	The **B** section appears in a transposed version, opening in D major and modulating to the home key (A major).
A	70–92	The *main theme* and its repetition are presented in an elaborately varied setting with added figuration and ornamentation, the aforementioned dynamic contrasts still intact. The movement is extended slightly by a *coda* (86–92).

Mozart's autograph of Sonata in D Major, *K. 284, first movement, mm. 1–20*

3rd Movement 102

Key: D major
Tempo: **Andante**
Time signatures: ₵, ¾
Form: theme and 12 variations (each section in two-part form with each part repeated)

Section	Measures	Analysis
Theme	1–17	A *theme* consisting of RH quarter and eighth notes with a LH eighth-note accompaniment unfolds in two parts, each marked to be repeated. The first part ends in the dominant (A major); the second part returns to the home key (D major).
Var. I	17–34	The two-part form of the theme is followed. The RH is varied with eighth-note triplets, marking the beginning of a *rhythmic crescendo*, the technique of using smaller note values to effect more rapid movement, a device that will be used for the next several variations.
Var. II	34–51	Using the two part-form, this variation presents LH eighth-note triplets and RH intermittent 16th notes that continue the rhythmic crescendo.
Var. III	51–68	Using the two part-form, this variation presents RH 16th notes throughout that continue the rhythmic crescendo.
Var. IV	68–85	The two-part form of the theme is followed. With 16th-note patterns in the LH opening and then in both hands, the rhythmic crescendo that began in Variation I comes to an end.
Var. V	85–102	The two-part form of the theme is followed, varied by a repeated-note figure in the RH and a double-3rd accompaniment in the LH.
Var. VI	102–119	Using the two part-form, this variation presents a LH that alternates between playing octaves and crossing over the RH for melodic fragments, while the RH maintains a 16th-note accompaniment pattern.
Var. VII	119–136	The two-part form of the theme is followed, but the tonality is the parallel minor (D minor), with the first part ending in A minor. The RH melody is interspersed with short trills.
Var. VIII	136–153	The two-part form of the theme is followed, and the tonality returns to the home key. Octave and double-3rd patterns appear in both hands.
Var. IX	153–170	Using the two part-form, this variation presents imitative two-note slurs and octave patterns that appear throughout.
Var. X	170–187	Using the two part-form, this variation begins with 16th-note tremolos in the RH that move to the LH and then into both hands.
Var. XI	187–221	This *Adagio cantabile* variation features an altered structure, each section repeat written out with elaborate figural and ornamental additions, creating the so-called "double variation."
Var. XII	221–260	This final *Allegro* variation features an altered structure, each section repeat written out to incorporate brilliance in the repeat. The second section is extended for increased excitement to close the movement.

Sonata in C Major

Wolfgang Amadeus Mozart (1756–1791)
K. 279

ⓐ Arpeggios in this movement should be played with the lowest note of each arpeggio *on the beat*.

ⓑ or *See also* mm. 4, 14, 15, 59, 61, 84, and 85.

ⓒ The grace notes in mm. 5, 6, and 62 should be played rapidly *before the beat* as crushed notes.

ⓓ or

ⓔ Performed *on the beat*, like the Baroque "slide":

ⓕ *See also* mm. 12, 20, 21, 36, 75, 76, 79, 80, and 97.

g *See also* mm. 14, 68, and 69.

h

i Although the grace notes in m. 16 may be played rapidly *before the beat*, execution *on the beat* as 16th notes may create a melodic idea that leads more naturally into the grace-note arpeggio in the following measure. *See also* mm. 18, 70, and 72.

j The grace-note arpeggio in m. 17 should be played as a 32nd-note triplet *on the beat*. *See also* mm. 19, 70, and 73.

k The staccato marks on the first set of 16th notes in m. 22 should probably attend the similar patterns in the second half of the measure and in mm. 23, 77, and 78. The realization of the trill in m. 22 should be adapted to mm. 23, 77, and 78.

l  Starting the trill on the main note in m. 25 seems logical in view of the repetition of the melodic idea in m. 26. *See also* m. 86.

m The playful spirit of mm. 26–30 is exemplified by the contrasting dynamic markings within mm. 28 and 29. This character suggests rapid single and double grace notes *before the beat*. *See also* mm. 87–90.

See also m. 91. For a discussion of the execution of cadential trills, see "Ornamentation and Improvisation" on pp. 7–9.

See also m. 46.

ⓟ *See also* m. 51.

ⓠ The 1841 André edition shows

(s) The RH slur on the 16th notes on beat 1 suggests a fingering that places the thumb on the first 16th note of beat 2. However, this fingering leads to a stretched hand position that will be too extended for some performers' hands. *See also* m. 73.

(t) The **f** mark in m. 77 is in both early sources but may be misplaced. Perhaps it should be at the start of the RH sequence in the preceding measure.

ⓤ The 1841 André edition shows the RH playing the first set of four 16th notes and the LH playing the second set.
The 1799 edition and most others reverse these hand positions.

30

(a) The triplet pulse throughout this movement and its notation open the question as to whether or not to assimilate duple notational patterns into the triplets. Should there be a polyrhythm between the hands, or should the melody rhythmically align with the LH triplet? *See* m. 2, beat 3. The earlier practice of rhythmic alteration was commonplace. However, the period in which this movement was written is one in which this practice was eroding. Contemporary treatises differ in their directions, some recommending it in rapid tempos but leaving the question open in slower tempos. Some editors recommend consistent assimilation throughout this movement, and some recorded performances follow this suggestion. Notice that this movement indicates duple-based upbeats of eighth notes and 16th notes with no clear, logical pattern. Also, polyrhythmic notation occurs occasionally, as in m. 16. Consequently, the variety with which Mozart notates upbeats may be an attempt to impart a feeling of freedom, even an improvisational spirit.

(b) The lyrical nature of this *Andante* suggests that grace notes be played *on the beat*, incorporating them into the melodic line. *See also* mm. 11, 12, 13, 43, and 51–53.

(c)  *See also* m. 55.

(d)  or

See also m. 56.

C. P. E. Bach might recommend

(e) The notation of 16th-note double-3rd appoggiaturas seems to be at odds with the two-note-slur patterns of the preceding and following three-measure groups, mm. 18–20 and 22–24. (*See also* m. 63 and its neighboring measures.) Many performers and editors realize this notation as it appears: as 16th-note appoggiaturas played *on the beat*, thus rendering the rhythm of the slurred notes differently from the triplet rhythms in the preceding and following measures. Others have suggested that the puzzling notation is simply the tradition of differently notating the dissonance that results for each of the three-note groups (created between the hands). This realization aligns the resolutions of the RH appoggiaturas with the first octave of the LH two-note groups, an alignment that is both logical and musical:

See also m. 67.

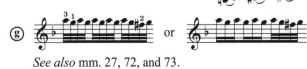

See also mm. 27, 72, and 73.

34

(c) The autograph is inconsistent in its slur markings of mm. 35, 36, 121, and 122. Only m. 35 shows a single slur over eight 16th notes. The other measures show two slurs over four-note groupings of 16th notes. Some editors regard this inconsistency as a slip of the pen by the composer and adjust the slurring one way or the other.

(d) Pianistic ease suggests the grace notes in mm. 38–44 be played rapidly *before the beat*, especially those attending the repeated eighth notes starting in m. 40. *See also* mm. 87 and 124–130.

(e) The autograph shows some inconsistency in the placement of the mark *p* in both RH and LH in mm. 47, 51, 148, and 152, sometimes showing the dynamic marking midway between the eighth notes of the second beat and sometimes clearly on the last eighth note of the measure. Historic editions have shown the placement differently, but most recent editions favor placing the mark on the second of the two eighth notes throughout.

f The second eighth note in the LH of m. 96 is shown as E 𝄢 in the autograph.

All editors change it to G 𝄢 .

g The RH slurring on the second beats of mm. 97–102 is represented as it appears in the autograph: some slurred in groups of four, others in groups of two. Some editors have deemed the seeming inconsistency as erroneous and have altered it in various ways.

(h) The autograph shows no G in the RH chord on the second beat.

(There is a small mark that looks more like a line than a note.) The 1841 André edition and others add the G to the chord.

Sonata in F Major

Wolfgang Amadeus Mozart (1756–1791)
K. 280

(a) The arpeggio should be played with the lowest note of the arpeggio *on the beat:*
See also mm. 7, 10, 48, 69, 71, 73, 75–77, 83, 89, 92, and 136.

(b) *See also* m. 84.

© *See also* mm. 43–46, 48–50, 130–134, and 136–138.

ⓓ *See also* m. 130.

ⓔ The first note of the ornament in m. 47 will be played by the LH as the upper note of its part. *See also* m. 135. In mm. 53 and 141, the first note of the ornament will be played by the RH, and the fingering of the final 16th note will be 2 instead of 5.

ⓕ *See also* mm. 142 and 143.

(a) Where to start the trill might well be a matter of preference, but many performers choose to start the trill on the main note, rather than on the upper auxiliary note, possibly because establishing the tonality of the movement is deemed more important than a melodic dissonant-to-consonant inflection. *See also* mm. 25, 33, and 37.

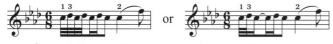

(b)  The RH grace notes in mm. 19, 20, 45, 49, and 54 should be played expressively as 16th-note appoggiaturas.

(c)

ⓓ   The arpeggio should be played with the lowest note *on the beat*.

(a) Play the grace notes in mm. 2–4, 10–12, 109–111, and 117–119 rapidly *before the beat*.

(b) Historical writings show disagreement as to the performance of the grace notes in the motive that appears first in mm. 38 and 39. C. P. E. Bach realizes the two-note slide *on the beat*, as do other conservative writers of the period. However, there is ample evidence that playing the two grace notes *before the beat* was also practiced and acknowledged. In this case, playing them *before the beat* facilitates preserving the dotted rhythm of the motive, so it seems appropriate to do so throughout the movement. For detailed information about this issue consult Rosenblum, pp. 234–239.

See also m. 160.

(d) The lowest note of the arpeggio should be played *on the beat*. *See also* m. 188.

(e) Measure 115 of the autograph shows a single slur attending the RH 16th notes, inconsistent with the slurring of m. 8.

48

Sonata in B-flat Major

Wolfgang Amadeus Mozart (1756–1791)

K. 281

(a) Where to start the trill might well be a matter of preference, but many performers choose to start the trill on the main note, rather than on the upper auxiliary note, possibly because establishing the tonality of the movement is deemed more important than a melodic dissonant-to-consonant inflection. *See also* mm. 5, 45, 70, and 74.

(b) In accordance with most period sources, arpeggios should be played rapidly with the lowest note *on the beat*. This would apply to the RH arpeggios in mm. 3, 54, 67, 68, and 72. Left-hand arpeggios presumably would follow this practice, although there is less consensus among performers when arpeggios are in the LH. The LH arpeggios in mm. 7, 47, 63, 65, and 76 will seem more pianistic to many performers if they are played rapidly *before the beat*, the top note of the arpeggio arriving *on the beat*. On the other hand, it could be argued that in these cases the lowest notes form intervals with the RH that are extensions of 3rds or 6ths and are thus richer harmonically.

(c) Play the grace notes in mm. 4 and 73 very rapidly *before the beat*.

(d) The grace notes in mm. 7, 29, 33, 47, 76, 98, and 102 are shown consistently as 32nd-note ornaments in the autograph. Each should be played as a 32nd note, resulting in groups of four equal 32nd notes.

See also mm. 25, 92, and 94. The easier version may be useful for some performers, albeit its 32nd notes render the after-notes rhythmically inaccurate.

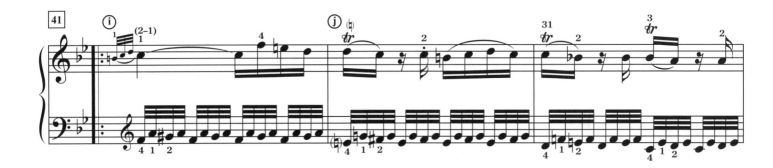

(f) The two grace notes on the downbeats of mm. 31 and 100 are written as 32nd notes. Being consonant with the underlying harmony but not written as full-sized notes suggests a more rapid execution, possibly as 64th notes. Playing these grace notes rapidly *on the beat* might be arguably more in keeping with period-performance practice; however, playing them rapidly *before the beat* highlights the interval of a 10th on the downbeat (between the melody and bass note), suggesting that the execution *before the beat* was intended.

(g) Play the grace notes on the second beats of mm. 33 and 102 rapidly *before the beat*.

(h)  *See also* m. 102.

(i)  The autograph shows the three grace notes before the downbeat of m. 41 as 32nd notes. It is recommended, however, that they be played as triplet 64th notes *on the beat*.

(j) *See also* mm. 43 and 44.

The harmonic progression in m. 58 suggests that starting trills on main notes is appropriate. Another issue is that the autograph is slightly smudged on the second set of LH 32nd notes, looking as if the second and third notes of the set might read F-sharp and G. The pattern in m. 60 is clear, however, and makes harmonic sense. Most editors alter the earlier measure.

Added after-notes to this ornament help smooth the line and are pianistic. *See also* m. 60.

(a) *See also* m. 65.

(b) *See* footnote (b) of the first movement for commentary on the performance of arpeggios.

(c) The autograph shows the grace notes in mm. 17, 19, 24, 25, 75, 77, 79, 84, and 85 as ♪. Play them rapidly *before the beat*. Although the grace notes in mm. 33, 37, 93, and 97 are written similarly in the autograph, their context as the first note of a descending scalar line leads most performers to play them as the first of six equal 16th notes.

ⓓ *See also* mm. 38, 40, 42, 94, 98, 100, and 102.

ⓔ The autograph shows beat 3 as ![notation], although m. 102 does not have an analogous interval at the end of the triplet.

Most editions omit the C from the LH interval in m. 42.

See also mm. 50 and 52.

The autograph clearly shows a different articulation in m. 68 from that of m. 10.

(a) The grace notes in mm. 1 and 2 should be played as eighth notes, the descending four eighth notes being of equal value. *See also* recurrences of the theme at mm. 44, 72, 115, and 143.

(b) *See also* mm. 38, 50, 78, 135, and 149. In m. 135, the first note of the ornament will be played by the LH as the upper note of its part.

(c) The grace notes in m. 17 should be played rapidly *before the beat. See also* mm. 19, 21, 88, 89, 101, 103, and 159–162.

(d) *See also* m. 20.

(e) The autograph shows the *p* indications in mm. 19 and 21 slightly to the right of the quarter notes on the downbeats. This has led to discrepancies in subsequent editions: some place the *p* on the downbeat, while others place it on beat 2.

(f) The autograph clearly shows [musical notation]. Most editors deem the B-flat an error and substitute G; a few do not.

(g) The grace note in m. 28 should be played rapidly *before the beat*. *See also* mm. 30, 124, and 126.

(h) Although period-performance practice might mandate that these grace notes be played rapidly *on the beat*, doing so in mm. 29 and 31 nearly creates parallel octaves between the hands. To avoid this parallelism, the editor suggests that the grace notes be played very rapidly *before the beat*. *See also* mm. 95, 99, and 125. The LH pattern changes in m. 127, so parallelism is not a concern, but use the same execution for consistency.

(i) [musical notation] or [musical notation]   The autograph shows an unusual symbol [musical notation] above the downbeats of mm. 30 and 126: [musical notation].

Although this unusual symbol is open to different interpretations, editorial consensus is that it is Mozart's version of a turn symbol with the addition of a slash through it. In rapid tempos, according to period-performance practice, the turn begins on the upper auxiliary and consists of four notes. However, many performers begin with the main note, making the turn consist of five notes. The slash may be an indication of this latter approach, to start on the main note. *See also* footnote (c) for the second movement of K. 284.

(j)    *See also* m. 130.

See also mm. 41, 42, 136, 137, 138, and 139.

63

See also m. 70.

Play the trill without after-notes, which maintains clarity in the contrary motion between the RH and LH lines.

(o) The rapidity of the long trills depends on the tempo taken for the overall movement. At a brisk overall tempo, 16th-note trills suffice. At a slower tempo, triplet 16th notes are possible. The LH trill should end on beat 4 of m. 122, since the RH and LH lines would otherwise collide.

(p) The arpeggio should be played *on the beat*.

Sonata in E-flat Major

Wolfgang Amadeus Mozart (1756–1791)
K. 282

(a) The grace note should be played *on the beat*, resulting in a group of four equal 16th notes.

(b)

(c)  Play double and triple grace notes *on the beat*.
See also mm. 5, 6, 15, and 33.

(d)  or   *See also* mm. 6, 14, and 32.

68

(e) The autograph shows single grace notes in this movement with slashes through their stems. Although playing grace notes *on the beat* was often the practice of the time, consider playing the grace notes *before the beat*: in mm. 13 and 31, to outline clearly the rising scalar line; in m. 17, to enhance the major to minor harmonic shift; and in mm. 22 and 23, for rhythmic clarity. Measure 35 lends itself to either execution. The cadence grace note in m. 36 is best realized as a 16th note *on the beat*, the following eighth note becoming a 16th as well.

(f) The position of the *p* markings in m. 16 reflects the autograph. While some editors move the *p* to the downbeat, others contend the autograph is correct and that the downbeat of m. 16 represents the culmination of the rising figure of m. 15.

(g)

Menuetto I

(a) The autograph shows the articulation of the opening theme as having three staccato quarter notes. This is consistent for mm. 3, 4, and 19–21. (The staccato is missing from the downbeat of m. 22.) These marks are only on the leading voice, never on accompanying voices. There is a performance tradition of playing the notes on the downbeats longer than those on beats 2 and 3. There are no markings on the quarter notes in mm. 9, 10, 27, or 28. Performers differ as to whether to play these notes staccato, reflecting the opening motive, or longer, relating them to the quarter notes in the following cadence measures.

(b) The broken chords should be played rapidly with the lowest note of each RH chord *on the beat*.

(c) The grace notes in mm. 16, 45 (beat 1), 46, 69 (beat 1), and 70 should be played as eighth notes.

(d) The LH fermata is an indication that at the end of the *da capo* the quarter note on the downbeat should be prolonged and the second quarter note should not be played.

Menuetto I da capo

ⓔ The grace notes in mm. 44, 45 (beat 3), 47, 68, 69 (beat 3), and 71 should be played as 16th notes, resulting in groups of four equal 16th notes.

(a) The grace note should be played as a 16th note, resulting in a group of four equal 16th notes.
See also mm. 7, 22, 30, 31, 34, 64, 68, 83, 91, and 95.

(b)  *See also* m. 11.

(c) *See also* mm. 70, 72, and 73.

(d) The arpeggios in mm. 20, 21, 28, 29, 81, 82, 89, and 90 should be played with the lowest note *on the beat*. The autograph clearly shows the lower notes of each chord as quarter notes, and the lowest note with a downward stem. Obviously, Mozart was thinking of voice levels, with the uppermost voice being longer and most prominent.

Sonata in G Major

Wolfgang Amadeus Mozart (1756–1791)
K. 283

(a) The suggested realizations are only two possibilities. Performers use a variety of realizations: a mordent, inverted mordent, turn or trill (starting on the main note or upper note), and a short trill with a lower after-note. Performers even vary the realization in the repeat of the exposition or in the recapitulation (m. 89).

(b) The grace notes in mm. 37, 42, 57, 59, 61 (beat 3), 104, and 109 should be played as 16th notes, resulting in groups of four equal 16th notes.

(c) *See also* mm. 44, 110, and 111.

ⓓ The autograph shows the grace notes in mm. 54, 56, 58, 60, and 61 (beat 1) as ♪. Performances differ as to their length.
Some performers play them *before the beat*, while others prefer a longer, more lyrical treatment *on the beat*,
notably those in mm. 54, 58, and 60.

ⓔ The autograph shows the grace notes in mm. 80 and 83 as ♪. Performance tradition is virtually unanimous for realizing these grace notes as eighth notes *on the beat*.

(a) The autograph shows the grace note as ♪. Tradition is strong for playing this grace note as a 16th note, equal in length to the following three 16th notes, maintaining a smooth lyrical line. *See also* mm. 4, 11, 12, 18, 19, 26, 28, 35, 36, and 41. Similarly, the grace notes attending 32nd notes appear as ♪ in the autograph. They, too, should be realized as equal notes with their following 32nd notes in mm. 13, 16, 17, 23, and 37.

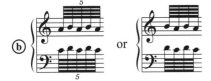 Most performers start the double trill in m. 2 with the main note. However, starting with the upper note is appropriate in this configuration and is less hurried. *See also* m. 26.

 *See also* mm. 12, 30, and 36.

(d) The inconsistency in the LH downbeats of mm. 14 and 15 are shown in the autograph and have been preserved in the text, despite the unison that results between the hands in m. 14.

Alternatively, start on the upper auxiliary, which creates an expressive dissonance with the D-sharp in the LH, one that is reiterated in m. 23 with the LH and the highest note of the RH phrase. If starting on the upper auxiliary, replace the two-note 32nd group at the end of the trill with a triplet.

Presto

(a) The tempo limits the trill to a three-note triplet. *See also* mm. 5, 172, and 176.

(b) The autograph shows the grace notes in mm. 4, 8, 34, 36, 38, 175, 179, 205, 207, and 209 as ♪. They can be played rapidly *on the beat* or *before the beat*.

ⓒ The autograph shows a discrepancy in the slurring of the three-note motive of the second theme in mm. 41–56 and mm. 212–227. In the earlier passage, the motive is slurred in groups of three, except for mm. 41 and 42 slurred in a group of six. The latter passage consistently shows six-note groupings, although sometimes shown only in the tenor voice.

ⓓ *See also* mm. 80, 137, 163, 167, 243, and 251.

Sonata in D Major

Wolfgang Amadeus Mozart (1756–1791)

K. 284

(a) The RH arpeggios throughout the movement should be played rapidly with the lowest note *on the beat*.
The grace notes on beats 3 and 4 should be played as 16th notes, resulting in groups of four even 16ths.
See also mm. 18, 20, 29–32, 36, 37, 72, 89, 91, 101–103, and 109.

(b) The autograph shows a discrepancy between the eighth-note slurs in m. 22 (a single slur) and m. 93 (pairs of eighths are under separate slurs). Editors handle this discrepancy in various ways: letting the difference stand, as shown in the autograph; adopting one of the patterns to both measures; or using double slurs.

(c) *See also* m. 94.

(d) The difference in articulation between mm. 27 and 99 (beats 3 and 4) is found in the autograph.

(e) The eighth-note upbeats to beats 1 and 3 in mm. 34–36 and 106–108 are often represented with different articulation patterns. The autograph shows but one staccato mark, on the eighth-note upbeat to beat 3 of m. 106. This has resulted in a variety of representations, ranging from staccato notes on all of the upbeats, to some, to none.

See also mm. 125.

ⓖ The first edition shows the RH chord on beat 2 as

(h) Throughout this sonata, dynamics in a smaller font are from the first edition but do not appear in the autograph.

Most editors deem this an error and use the autograph version, as represented in this edition.

Rondeau en Polonaise

Andante

(a) In mm. 5 and 6, the autograph shows ***f*** markings in both measures at the entrance of the RH 32nd notes, while the first edition shows ***sfp***. Editorial representations of this seeming discrepancy vary. In both measures, the RH first-beat note and LH second-beat chord should be played ***p***. The rest of the measure should be played ***f***, with an accent on the first of the RH 32nd notes.

The autograph shows [chord notation] as the LH chord on beat 3 of m. 5.

This edition follows the first edition. The D is probably a slip of the pen on the composer's part, inasmuch as the doubling with the RH D is unlikely. One can note also that the bass figuration in m. 74 contains the E.

(b) All single grace notes in this movement appear in the autograph as ♪. Those in mm. 12–14, 18, 20, 54, and 56 may be played either rapidly *before the beat* or as a 16th note *on the beat*. Contemporary performers use either but are consistent in applying whatever is selected throughout these measures.

(c) [ornament notation] The autograph shows three different ornament signs in mm. 17–20 and 53–56: the 𝆕 (trill), the mordent, and an unusual one believed to be a mordent with a slash through it. (*See also* footnote ⓘ for the third movement of K. 281.) The latter opens the sequence in m. 17, while the trill opens the sequences in mm. 19 and 53. Mordents are used for other decorated notes in the passage. The first edition, however, shows only the trill indication throughout these passages. Editions represent these ornaments in a variety of ways. This edition includes the autograph version with the first edition ornaments in parentheses. However, ornamentation was improvised in this period, and differences in symbols do not necessarily represent fixed performance directions. Contemporary performers often use but one ornament consistently throughout the two passages, usually the five-note ornament realized above.

(d) Many editors suggest adding double-sharps to the LH F's in mm. 19 and 73, as well as the B's in m. 55, although neither the autograph nor the first editions show them.

(e) Sixteenth-note execution *on the beat* is recommended for the grace notes in mm. 31 and 33.

(f)   *See also* m. 36.

(g) The grace notes should be played as 16th notes, resulting in a group of four even 16th-note 3rds.

The first edition shows LH octaves

(h) The autograph shows the slur attending the lower voice of beat 3 extending to the bar line but stopping short of the *f* mark on

the downbeat of m. 47. This ambiguity could be interpreted as  .

(i) [music example] or [music example] *See also* m. 49.

See also m. 72. Starting the trill on the upper note would follow the Leopold Mozart treatise. (*See* p. 8.) However, the return of the main theme of this movement has influenced many performers to start these trills on the main note. If starting on the upper note, use the same triplet rhythm with a full triplet at the end. In the spirit of improvisation, some performers have started the trill in m. 70 on the main note and the one in m. 72 on the upper note.

The RH ornaments in mm. 74 and 75 are examples of the unusual sign that is open to interpretation. (*See* footnote ⓒ for this movement and footnote ⓘ for the third movement of K. 281.) In this passage, the ornament represents a turn that begins on the principle note. Both the placement of the ornaments and the difference in RH tied notes in these two measures reflect the autograph. Some editors have speculated that the two measures should be congruous.

102

(a) The autograph has no tempo indication. The first edition shows *Andante*.

(b) Differences in phrase groups between the autograph and the first edition occur frequently throughout this movement. The main text follows the autograph; footnotes describe first edition markings. In mm. 2 and 15, the first four eighth notes in the RH are under a single phrase mark.

(c) In Variation I, the first edition shows the following phrasing: m. 18, RH triplets under a single phrase; m. 21, RH triplets on beat 2 phrased in two groups of three; m. 22, RH triplets on beat 1 in two groups of three, but on beat 2 the triplets under one phrase; m. 23, RH triplets in two groups of six; m. 25 upbeat after the double bar, triplets in one group of six; m. 26, LH shows no phrasing; m. 27, each of the RH triplets shows the first two notes slurred and the third one with a staccato; m. 28, RH triplets under one phrase; m. 31, RH triplets under one phrase; and m. 32, RH triplets in two groups of six.

ⓓ The double grace notes in Variation II appear in the autograph as small 32nd notes. They should be played rapidly *on the beat*.

(e) The grace notes should be played as 16th notes, resulting in groups of four even 16th notes.

(f) The autograph clearly shows a staccato mark on the first quarter note. This upbeat half-measure appears revised, for it has the look of something having been scratched out and the first note with its staccato written in a darker shade over whatever was rejected. However, neither the RH quarter note that immediately follows nor the quarter notes in mm. 72, 76, 81, or 85 show staccatos. Editors sometimes add staccato marks to quarter notes in measures where similar articulation might seem logical.

Arpeggios in mm. 69, 73, 76, 82, and 85 should be played rapidly with the lowest note *on the beat*. The notation of upper notes as half notes and lower notes as quarter notes in mm. 69, 73, and 82 appears in the autograph, probably a device to ensure upper-note prominence.

(g) Most editors suggest the double-sharps, likely inadvertently omitted from the autograph. *See also* m. 75, beat 2.
Similarly, sharps are often applied in m. 78 to LH and RH D's, beats 2 and 3; however, such additions are less certain.

(h)

ⓘ The grace notes in mm. 93 and 102 are shown in the autograph as ♪. Play them rapidly *before the beat*.

ⓙ In Variation VI, the autograph shows staccato marks only on the three quarter-note octaves that form the upbeats/downbeat to mm. 103, 107, and 115. Editors sometimes add staccatos to the LH pattern from m. 115 to 116.

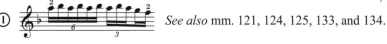

(k) The first edition shows the last three 16th notes in m. 109 as [notation].

(l) [notation] *See also* mm. 121, 124, 125, 133, and 134.

(m) The autograph clearly shows a C-sharp as the penultimate RH 16th note of m. 125. However, many editors believe a C-double-sharp should be used instead.

Var. VIII

(n) The autograph shows staccato marks on the first five RH notes of Variation IX and on the last two eighth notes in m. 161. It is probably safe to assume that the motive stated in m. 161 and the first two RH eighth notes of m. 162 should have staccato marks since they reflect the opening motive of this variation. Many editors add staccato markings to the eighth-note octaves throughout this variation, an addition the composer perhaps thought unnecessary, for given the tempo of the octaves and the absence of phrase marks, the octaves will likely sound detached anyway.

(o) The RH figure consisting of the eighth note and the following quarter at the end of m. 164 is shown in the autograph with both a staccato mark on the eighth note and a phrase mark connecting the eighth note to the quarter note. The first edition shows only the phrase mark, which is consistent with the earlier representation of this figure in the variation.

(p) The repeats of the 11th variation are written out by the composer, displaying different improvisatory treatments of the music. The first edition shows still another version of the variation. The two versions exemplify the improvisatory flexibility performers were allowed, even expected, to use in playing music of this period. Such creativity was especially appropriate in performing slow movements, where the tempo allowed for greater variation. Thus the footnoted realizations represent a conservative approach, one that invites more elaborate improvisation.

(q)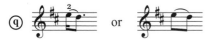

An interesting detail that exemplifies the improvisational attitude with which ornaments were realized is that the autograph shows the RH grace note on the downbeat of m. 188 as ♪, whereas the ones at mm. 196 and 209 are each shown as ♪, while m. 218 shows the idea written out (in normal-sized notes) with two 16th notes followed by a quarter note.

(r)

(s) The RH grace note in m. 189 is shown in the first edition as a small 32nd note, to be played *on the beat*:

(t)    (v)  This four-note realization should be adapted to the grace-note pattern in mm. 194, 195, 200, and 202.

(u)    (w)  or

The first edition shows the RH grace notes as 32nd notes, in which case they might be played as shown in the realization. The autograph shows ♪, a representation that suggests they be played rapidly *before the beat*.

Var. XII
(Allegro)

(uu) The autograph shows the RH notes at the beginning of mm. 222, 226, and 243 as ♪, suggesting that they be played rapidly *before the beat*. The first edition shows two regular eighth notes in each case, a version this editor prefers.

(vv) Arpeggios in mm. 227, 256, 258, and 260 should be played rapidly with the lowest note *on the beat*.

(ww) The figure that begins in the LH in m. 230 and continues throughout this variation often appears in the autograph without accidentals that some editors have deemed appropriate. These possible omissions are shown in parentheses in the LH in mm. 230, 236, 252, 256, and 258, and in the RH in m. 249.

The autograph of the K. 309 is not extant. There is an autograph in another handwriting, believed to be that of the composer's father, Leopold, possibly made near the beginning of 1778. The first edition is part of a set of three keyboard sonatas published by Franz Joseph Heina (1729–1790) in Paris sometime after Mozart left that city in the early fall of 1778, the publication appearing possibly as late as 1782. The set also contained K. 310 and K. 311. Heina had befriended Mozart during his stay in Paris and offered support when the composer's mother became ill and later passed away. Heina published several first editions of the composer's music, including sets of variations for keyboard K. 179, K. 180, and K. 354. While Leopold's autograph is assumed to be reasonably accurate, the first edition is rife with obvious errors, as well as inconsistencies in dynamics and articulation. The engraver identified on the cover of the three sonatas is one Mlle. Fleury. The apparent carelessness Fleury exhibits in the set of three sonatas is, strangely, not consistent with other extant examples of her work. Some have speculated that the autograph from which she worked was prepared by yet another copyist, possibly hired by the composer. Even with so many obvious errors, the first edition cannot be completely discounted, and scholars have gleaned information from both it and the aforementioned autograph. Inasmuch as the number of issues between these two sources is so great, this edition notes only differences deemed important to the performer by this editor. Some of these differences are indicated in footnotes; dynamics in smaller typeset appear only in the first edition.

Castle (Prospect of the Electoral Palace of Mannheim) (ca. 1780) By Georg Balthasar Probst (German, 1732–1801) Engraving

The K. 309 sonata is believed to have been completed in Mannheim in late October of 1777, when the composer and his mother were on their way to Paris. Mannheim was famous for its orchestra, supported from 1740 to 1788 by Elector Karl Theodor (1724–1799). Moreover, the city also became known for musical characteristics associated with the composers who wrote for the orchestra. In a letter dated December 11, 1777, Leopold wrote to his son, describing K. 309 as "strange" with the comment that it "has something in it of the rather artificial Mannheim style, but so very little that your own good style is not spoilt."[18] In an earlier letter dated December 8, 1777, Mozart's sister, Anna Maria ("Nannerl"), adds a postscript commenting, "I like the style very much. One can see from its style that you composed it in Mannheim."[19] Evidence of the Mannheim influence is the *forte* unison opening, imitating an orchestral texture that must have been overwhelming to the listeners of the time. There is as well Mozart's description of the second movement as a portrait of the 15-year-old daughter of the orchestra's conductor, Christian Cannabich (1731–1798). In a letter dated December 6, 1777, Mozart described Rose (1764–1839) as "pretty . . . charming . . . intelligent . . . amiable . . . She is exactly like the Andante."[20]

---

18 Anderson, *The Letters of Mozart and His Family*, 417.
19 Ibid., 412.
20 Ibid., 408.

SONATA IN C MAJOR, K. 309

1st Movement 121

Key: C major
Tempo: **Allegro con spirito**
Time signature: **C**
Form: sonata-allegro (with sections repeated)

Section	Measures	Analysis
Exposition	1–20	After a unison opening (1 and 2), staccato repeated quarter notes and octaves in the RH form a melodic line with a LH accompaniment in eighth notes (3–20).
	21–34	A *transition* opens in C major and modulates to the dominant (G major).
	35–58	The *second theme* area in G major features RH staccato eighth notes answered by the rhythmic figures ♪♩ and ♪♩. (called *Lombard rhythm* or the *Scotch snap*) (35–42), and an extended final passage containing RH octaves, 16th notes, and trills (43–58). Within the final passage are noteworthy measures with contrasting *piano* and *forte* markings on every beat (48 and 49).
Development	59–85	The opening phrase of the *exposition* is stated, fragmented, and then answered by short lyrical RH segments, these ideas passing through several keys, including G minor, D minor, and A minor (59–82). A *transition* leads back to the home key using a three-note figure heard near the close of the *exposition* (82–85).
Recapitulation	86–155	The *exposition* material is repeated and slightly varied, the *second theme* area remaining in the home key (C major). A short extension features a reappearance of the opening phrase of the movement (152 and 153).

2nd Movement 128

Key: F major
Tempo: **Andante un poco adagio**
Time signature: **¾**
Form: **AA'BA"A'''** coda

Section	Measures	Analysis
A	1–16	The *main theme* is characterized by dotted rhythms. Its first eight measures are repeated with decorative changes, including additional grace notes and 32nd notes.
A'	17–32	The *main theme* is presented again with more elaborate ornamentation and additional decorative passagework. Grace notes and 32nd notes abound.
B	33–44	The contrasting **B** section features a RH melody in C major (33–40) dovetailing with a *transition* leading back to the home key (F major) (40–44).
A"	45–60	The *main theme* is presented once again, this time with RH octaves and scale-like passagework in 32nd notes.
A'''	60–79	A more ornamented version of the *transition* that appeared at the end of the **B** section serves as an introduction to the final statement of the *main theme* (60–64). The first eight measures of the **A** theme are stated in another varied form (65–72), the last four measures being repeated with variation and extended to form the *coda* (72–79).

Key: C major
Tempo: **Rondeau – Allegretto grazioso**
Time signature: $\frac{2}{4}$
Form: **ABACBA** coda

Section	Measures	Analysis
A	1–39	The *main theme* is stated with a LH accompaniment of broken triads in 16th notes, the first eight measures being repeated with small variations (1–19). Then, a *second section* opening with RH arpeggios and LH octaves acts as a transition to the dominant (G major) (19–39).
B	39–92	The **B** section opens in the dominant (G major) with RH passagework in 16th-note triplets (40–52). Then, a passage of RH melodic fragments comprised of repeated notes and dotted rhythms leads to an orchestral-like RH 32nd-note tremolo with both major and parallel minor inflections (52–77). A *closing section* acts as a transition, setting up the home key (C major) (77–92).
A	93–115	Only the first 15 measures of the *main theme* are repeated (93–107), for a *transition* section interrupts to set up the key of the next section and briefly brings back RH 32nd-note tremolos (108–115).
C	116–142	A *new theme* of 16 measures is stated in F major (116–131), followed by a *transition* section that brings back the RH 16th-note triplets and leads to the home key (C major).
B	142–188	The **B** section is restated in the home key. Instead of the closing section, the RH tremolos and triplets are extended, touching on D minor, and then set up the dominant of the home key.
A	189–244	The first 15 measures of the *main theme* are repeated (189–203), followed by inserted material from various earlier passages (triplet 16th notes, tremolos, etc.) (204–234). Then, the second section from the first appearance of the *main theme* returns (234–244).
Coda	244–252	The opening phrases of the *main theme* act as a *coda*.

The Mozart Family (ca. *1780)*
By Johann Nepomuk della Croce (Austrian, 1736–1819)
Oil on canvas

Sonata in C Major

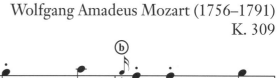

Wolfgang Amadeus Mozart (1756–1791)

K. 309

(a) Although not found in the autograph or first edition, the LH low C is usually added inasmuch as it appears in m. 8. The RH arpeggio should be played rapidly *on the beat*. *See also* mm. 8, 27, 28, 59, 67, 86, 90, 94, 101, and 152.

(b) Sources show the grace note as a small 16th note, and it should be played as such, rendering the first beat two equal 16th notes: . *See also* mm. 5, 11, 12, 97, 98, and 103.

(c) The grace note should be played as a 16th note, resulting in a group of four equal 16th notes: . *See also* mm. 20, 27, 28, 112, 115, and 146.

(d) *See also* mm. 20, 112, and 115.

(e) Although sources show the grace notes in mm. 21, 23, 25, 116, 118, and 120 with two or three flags and no slash, they should be played rapidly *before the beat*.

(f) The arpeggio signs are missing from Leopold Mozart's autograph from the RH chords in mm. 23, 25, 58, and 120. However, analogous mm. 118 and 155 show them.

g The second RH eighth note in m. 51 shows a staccato mark, perhaps indicating that the initial eighth note on the downbeat completes the preceding measure's idea while the second eighth note acts as an upbeat to the descending trills passage. The two-note slurs are not in Leopold Mozart's autograph but are found in the first edition and facilitate playing the trills. *See also* m. 145.

h *or* *See also* m. 147.

(i) *See also* m. 69.

(j) The difference in the notation of the LH between the passages starting at mm. 63 and 69 is in the sources, but there would seem to be very little audible difference in the two.

(k) The grace notes should be played rapidly *before the beat*, thus supporting the harmonic resolution.

(l) Play the arpeggios in mm. 81 and 82 rapidly *on the beat*.

126

ⓜ Some later editions show the last eighth note in both the RH and LH with a sharp.

Andante un poco adagio

(a)   *See also* mm. 12.   (c)   *See also* mm. 15, 23, and 33.

(b)   (d)   *See also* mm. 31, 51, 71, and 75–77.

ⓔ The grace notes in mm. 17–19 should be played rapidly *before the beat*.

In m. 19, the first edition shows [musical example]. These substitutions are perhaps more pianistic than those shown in the autograph.

(f) The first edition shows

(g) *See also* m. 59.

(h) or

(i)

ⓙ The first edition shows [musical notation]. Some later editions show [musical notation] as beat 1 of m. 56.

ⓚ [musical notation]   ⓜ [musical notation]

ⓛ [musical notation]   ⓝ The first edition shows [musical notation].

(o) Several later editors were apparently troubled by the RH doubling of the 3rd of the implied harmony, substituting either F or C for the lower note of the RH interval.

(p) Play the RH grace note rapidly *before the beat*.

RONDEAU
Allegretto grazioso

(a) The rhythmic pattern ♪♩ ♪♪ is presented throughout this movement as an integral part of its main themes. It should be played as four 16th notes.

(b) Play the three-note ornament rapidly *on the beat*. *See also* mm. 12, 190, and 192.

(c) or *See also* mm. 107 and 203.

ⓔ   The grace notes can be played rapidly *on the beat* or *before the beat*. *See also* m. 167.

ⓕ The grace note may be played either *before the beat* or as a 16th note *on the beat* as shown. *See also* mm. 68, 170, and 172.

ⓖ Play the arpeggios in mm. 76, 77, and 86–88 rapidly with the lowest note *on the beat*.

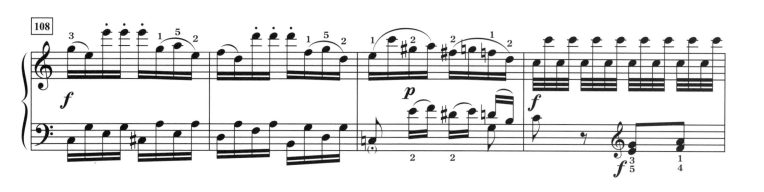

(h) There is a performance tradition of realizing the grace notes in m. 116 with the same rhythm as those in mm. 36 and 37. (*See* the realization in footnote (d).) The difference in notation, however, suggests that the grace notes in m. 116 should be played more rapidly as crushed notes before the first of each pair of 32nd notes. *See also* mm. 118, 120, 124, 126, 128, and 129.

(i) The LH accompaniment for this passage reflects the first edition and Leopold Mozart's copy. However, another version has appeared in a significant number of later editions with the following changes.

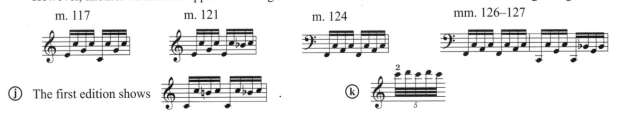

ⓛ *See also m. 200.*

ⓜ The Leopold Mozart autograph shows

ⓝ The grace note should be played as a 32nd note *on the beat*.

ⓞ *See also m. 220.*

142

(p) A significant number of later editions substitute E-flats in place of E-naturals in the RH chords of mm. 230 and 231, as well as the first 32nd note in m. 232. However, these changes are not in the sources.

(q) After Leopold Mozart. (*See* p. 8.)

About K. 310

Unlike many of the other keyboard sonatas, K. 310 is not mentioned in the composer's letters, so nothing is known of his thoughts about this important work. From autograph evidence, it was composed in Paris during the summer of 1778, the period when Mozart's mother, who was with him in Paris, became ill and passed away. That tragic, traumatic event in Mozart's life is often mentioned when referring to K. 310, probably because of the work's minor key (one of only two Mozart keyboard sonatas in minor) and an emotional intensity that many deem anguished.

The first edition of K. 310 was as part of a set of three sonatas published by Franz Joseph Heina in Paris sometime after Mozart left that city in the early fall of 1778, the publication appearing possibly as late as 1782. The set also contained K. 309 and K. 311. Heina had befriended Mozart during his stay in Paris and had offered support as Mozart endured his mother's death. Unfortunately, the first edition is rife with obvious errors, inconsistencies in dynamics and articulation, and even passages written in the wrong octave. (For more details regarding this engraving, *see* the introductory text to K. 309.) Fortunately, in the case of K. 310, the autograph has survived and can serve as a primary source. It is in the Morgan Library and Museum, New York, New York.

View of Paris *(1729)*
By Jacques Rigaud (French, 1680–1754)
Engraving

SONATA IN A MINOR, K. 310

Key: A minor
Tempo: **Allegro maestoso**
Time signature: ¢
Form: sonata-allegro (with sections repeated)

Section	Measures	Analysis
Exposition	1–22	A strong *opening theme* is comprised of a RH motive of quarter notes and dotted rhythms with LH repeated chords in eighth notes. A slightly varied version is stated in C minor with LH 16th notes, coming to rest on a half cadence (16–22).
	22–49	The *second theme* area is in C major, unfolding in continuous 16th-note passagework, first in the RH and then the LH. A *closing section* restates the rhythm of the *first theme* with a LH 16th-note accompaniment (45–49).
Development	50–79	The *first theme* is stated in C major and extended (50–57). Then, the rhythmic pattern of the *first theme* is combined with dotted rhythm fragments in imitative voice levels in the RH over a 16th-note accompaniment in the LH. This contrapuntal display is stated first in E minor, then in A minor, and finally in D minor (58–70). The resolution to D minor ushers in a *transition* section that sets up the dominant of the home key (70–79).
Recapitulation	80–133	The *exposition* material is restated with some variation (88–96 and 126–128), the *second theme* area remaining in the home key (A minor).

Key: F major
Tempo: **Andante cantabile**
Time signature: ¾
Form: sonata-allegro (with exposition repeated)

Section	Measures	Analysis
Exposition	1–14	The *first theme* unfolds in two sections: the first consisting of a lyrical melody in two four-measure segments (1–8); the second using more active motives in 16th and 32nd notes, encompassing a range of two octaves, over a LH broken-triad pattern (8–14).
	14–31	The *second theme* opens in C major with a section that features RH repeated 16th notes, a two-measure trill, and expressive four-note patterns marked *fp* (14–22). Then, the four-note pattern is transformed into RH phrases that open with 16th-note broken octaves and are extended into 32nd-note cadenza-like passagework, first in the RH and then in the LH, before closing with a C major cadence (22–31).
Development	31–53	The *development* opens with a gesture similar to that of the opening phrase of the movement. The lyrical phrase is then altered and extended (31–37). Then, the relationship between this section and material presented in the *exposition* becomes less clear, albeit the mood and drama of the section remains that typical of *development* sections. At m. 37, the LH ushers in broken 16th-note triplets as an accompaniment to a RH figure in eighth notes. At m. 43, the LH and RH roles are reversed, and the entire texture passes through a series of minor keys, including D minor, C minor, and G minor, before finally coming to rest on the dominant of the home key.
Recapitulation	53–86	The *recapitulation* presents all material heard in the *exposition*. A varied harmonic progression in mm. 62–67 sets up the arrival of the home key (F major) for the *second theme* area.

Key: A minor
Tempo: **Presto**
Time signature: 2/4
Form: **ABA** (**B** section in two parts, each repeated)

Section	Measures	Analysis
A	1–142	A two-note slurred motive consisting of a dotted quarter note followed by an eighth note opens in RH 3rds and permeates the movement, becoming especially prominent in the two **A** sections. There are many subsections in which this figure appears, sometimes answered by short eighth-note patterns: in F major leading to C major (20–28), in C minor (29–32), in parallel 4ths (37–51), in LH octaves (64–71) and double 3rds (72–86), and in RH double 3rds (127–142). Interspersed are short departures (52–59 and 87–106), as well as a return to the opening statement (107–127), which impart a rondo-like feeling to the section.
B	143–174	Opening in A major with phrases that reference the two-note motive of the **A** section, the first section cadences in the dominant (E major) and is marked to be repeated (143–158). The second section presents two four-measure phrases in RH eighth notes and then returns to phrases that reference the **A**-section rhythm. The section cadences in A major and is marked to be repeated (159–175).
A	176–253	The first 16 measures of the **A** section return. Then, new and tension-filled material unfolds, consisting of departures from and variations of the material heard in the first **A** section (196–253). A strong cadence with RH chords and LH repeated octaves closes the movement.

Sonata in A Minor

Wolfgang Amadeus Mozart (1756–1791)
K. 310

(a) The opening grace note is written as a small 16th note in the sources but is most frequently played rapidly *before the beat*. *See also* mm. 9 and 50.

(b) The grace notes on the downbeats of mm. 2, 4, 51, 53, 81, and 83 are most often realized as eighth notes. However, some performers believe they should be played as 16ths, perhaps reasoning that the grace-note realization should differ from the eighth-note motive appearing in mm. 10, 12, 15, 89, and 91.

(c) The grace notes in mm. 15, 33, 39, 44, 57, 115, 120, and 125 should be played as 16th notes, resulting in groups of four equal 16th notes.

ⓓ Play the arpeggios with the lowest note *on the beat*. *See also* mm. 49, 97, 99, and 103.

ⓔ After Leopold Mozart. (*See* page 8.) If starting the trill on the main note, incorporate the after-notes as a group of four 32nd notes. *See also* m. 115.

See also m. 120.

See also mm. 42 (beat 4), 43, 70–72, 74–77, 123, and 124.

(h) Many later editions show the downbeat of m. 76 as identical with that of m. 74. This edition reflects the first edition and autograph.

(i) It is unclear as to whether the grace note attending the downbeat of m. 1 should be repeated at the start of the recapitulation, given the last 16th note in m. 79. The autograph shows only *da capo* for the next eight measures. Some early editions show the grace note; later editions often exclude it.

(j) The autograph shows beats 3 and 4 as [musical example]. Traditionally, however, the E has been deemed erroneous and should be replaced by F in keeping with the RH pattern of mm. 90 and 91.

ⓐ The grace notes in mm. 1 and 54 are written as small 16th notes in the sources. Performers differ with regard to realization, some playing them rapidly *before the beat*, others playing them as 32nd notes *on the beat*, and a few playing them as 16th notes *on the beat*. Occasionally, performers add similar grace notes to the downbeats of mm. 5 and 58.

ⓑ The syncopated RH chord on the second half of beat 2 of mm. 3 and 56 is marked with an arpeggio sign. The syncopation is preserved more clearly if the uppermost note is played on the second half of beat 2 with the two lower notes preceding it.

ⓒ  The grace note should be realized as a 32nd note *on the beat. See also* mm. 7, 13, 58, and 60.

ⓕ  A trill of 64th notes incorporating the grace note and the after-notes as 32nds works well in mm. 7 and 60. *See also* mm. 21, 24, 76, and 79.

ⓓ  *See also* mm. 29 and 59.

ⓖ 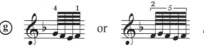 *See also* m. 61.

ⓔ

ⓗ  *See also* mm. 36 and 62.

See also mm. 20, 24, 35, 36, 60, 75, and 79.

Starting the trill on the main note
is appropriate inasmuch as its function
is to sustain the dominant tone rather than provide melodic
decoration. *See also* mm. 70 and 71.

See also m. 80.

Starting the trills in mm. 28 and 83 on the main note is appropriate inasmuch as their function is harmonic rather than melodic.

The *sf* suggests starting the ornament on the main note: . *See also* m. 84.

See also m. 85.

(p) The grace note should be played as a 16th note *on the beat*. *See also* mm. 34 and 36.

Most performers start the RH trills in mm. 37 and 39, as well as the second half of beat 2 in mm. 41 and 42, on the main note. The number of notes that can be used comfortably in these ornaments depends on the underlying tempo of the movement.

The grace-note appoggiatura in m. 39 suggests starting the trill at the beginning of m. 41 with the upper note. Performers, however, often prefer starting on the main note. *See also* mm. 51.

The suggested realizations of the LH trills in mm. 44, 46, 48, and 49 contain fewer notes in order to maintain clarity in the lower register of the keyboard. As in the preceding passage, most performers prefer beginning these trills on the main note (even when doing so requires a rapid repetition of the upbeat note).

See also m. 74.

(a) The grace note, written as a small 8th note followed by a quarter note, is an integral part of the thematic material throughout this movement. The grace note and its following main note should always be played as two equal eighth notes, slurred as a couplet. The grace note in m. 25 should be played rapidly *before the beat*.

(b)

<table>
<tr><td>About
K. 311</td><td>The exact composition date of K. 311 is uncertain. An unidentified sonata is mentioned in a letter the composer wrote to his cousin, Maria Anna Thekla (1758–1841), dated November 5, 1777, possibly this work.[21] If so, K. 311 predates K. 310, probably having been begun in Augsburg in the summer of 1777 and finished in the fall in Mannheim on the way to Paris.</td></tr>
</table>

The first edition of K. 311 was as part of a set of three sonatas published by Franz Joseph Heina in Paris sometime after Mozart left that city in the early fall of 1778, the publication appearing possibly as late as 1782. The set also contained K. 309 and K. 310. Heina had befriended Mozart during his stay in Paris and had offered support as Mozart endured his mother's death. Unfortunately, the first edition is rife with obvious errors, inconsistencies in dynamics and articulation, and even passages written in the wrong octave. (For more details regarding this engraving, *see* the introductory text to K. 309.) Fortunately, in the case of K. 311, the autograph has survived and can serve as a primary source. It is in the Biblioteka Jagiellońska, Kraków, Poland.

SONATA IN D MAJOR, K. 311

1st Movement 168

Key: D major
Tempo: **Allegro con spirito**
Time signature: 𝄵
Form: sonata-allegro (with sections repeated)

Section	Measures	Analysis
Exposition	1–16	Opening with a D major chord, the *first theme* presents RH melodic fragments over LH accompaniment patterns of 3rds and broken intervals (1–10), followed by RH passagework in 16th notes (11–16). A half cadence prepares the way for the dominant key (A major).
	16–39	The *second theme* area opens with RH eighth-note fragments that cadence in A major (16–24). Then, 16th-note accompaniment patterns support short phrases of eighth notes, the hands trading roles and the RH crossing over the LH at one point (24–36). Strong authentic cadences in A major followed by a lyrical phrase of double-6th two-note slurs end the section (36–39).
Development	40–57	The two-note slurs that appeared at the end of the *exposition* form the basis for the entire *development* section, moving through E minor and D minor, and coming to rest in B minor (40–55). Two measures of transition set up the key of G major (56 and 57).
Recapitulation	58–112	The *recapitulation* is unusual in that it changes the order of material heard in the *exposition* and adds new passagework. It opens by restating a portion of the *second theme* heard in mm. 28–35, now in the key of G major (58–65). Then, a flurry of new RH 16th-note passagework builds excitement and dovetails with the same half cadence heard in m. 16 (66–78). Then, the *second theme* area unfolds in the home key of D major as it did in the *exposition* (78–98), until interrupted by six measures of the *first theme* as it appeared in the opening of the movement (99–105). This restatement is extended with passagework. The *recapitulation* closes with the aforementioned strong cadences and two-note slurs, now in the home key of D major (106–112).

Mozart's autograph of Sonata in D Major, *K. 311, first movement, mm. 1–12*

---

[21] Anderson, 359.

2nd Movement 174

Key: G major
Tempo: **Andante con espressione**
Time signature: $\frac{2}{4}$
Form: **AABCABCA** coda

Section	Measures	Analysis
A	1–11	The *main theme* is stated in two four-measure phrase segments followed by a repeated cadential phrase, similar to a refrain or ritornello. The section is marked to be repeated.
B	12–24	Five measures of cadence-like transitional material lead to a *new theme* in the RH in D major, set in a high register in eighth and 16th notes and supported by LH 16th-note patterns.
C	25–38	The beginning of the **A** theme is presented in D major but does not unfold as in its original statement. Rather, its first two measures are repeated by the LH below a long RH trill (27 and 28), and then a three-note motive originally presented in m. 3 is varied, extended, and repeated (29–38).
A	39–50	The *main theme* is restated in G major with small ornamental variations.
B	50–60	The **B** section as heard earlier is repeated in the home key (G major).
C	61–74	The **C** section as heard earlier is repeated with small variations in the home key (G major).
A	75–93	The *main theme* is stated with figural variations, its refrain-like extension being repeated in RH octaves and extended to serve as a *coda*.

3rd Movement 178

Key: D major
Tempo: **Rondeau – Allegro**
Time signature: $\frac{6}{8}$
Form: rondo – **ABACABA**

Section	Measures	Analysis
A	1–18	The *main theme* divides the $\frac{6}{8}$ meter into two sets of three, providing a triplet-like energy to the RH melody in eighth notes, interspersed with 16th-note scalar passagework.
B	19–85	The lengthy **B** section opens with a transition that culminates in a strong modulation to the dominant key (19–32), followed by brilliant RH 16th-note passagework ending in a half cadence in A major (33–40). A lyrical thematic phrase in the RH is imitated by the LH and extended (41–55). Then, another section of RH passagework leads to two-note slurs (61), repeated in staccato octaves (72), and finally RH cadential phrases supported by LH 16th notes that set up the return to the *main theme* and the home key (D major) (75–85).
A	86–104	The *main theme* is repeated.
C	105–173	The material used earlier to lead to the **B** section serves as a transition to section **C** and sets up the key of B minor (105–118). A *new theme* in which the RH eighth notes are decorated periodically with trills is supported by LH 16th-note patterns. The hands then exchange material with extended passagework (118–138). A *second new theme* in G major appears briefly (139–156) and then dovetails with the transition material previously heard between sections, now serving to set up the return of the *main theme* in the home key (157–172). A written-out cadenza, without bar lines, is inserted before the return of the *main theme* (173). Suggesting improvisation, it is marked with tempo changes (*Andante*, *Presto*, and *Adagio*) and is interspersed with fermata signs.
A	173–189	The *main theme* is repeated.
B	189–248	After a varied version of the transitional material, the **B** section is repeated with small alterations in the home key (D major).
A	248–269	Eight measures of the *main theme* are repeated and followed by 11 measures of the transition material, now used to bring the movement to a close.

Mozart's autograph of Sonata in D Major, *K. 311, third movement, mm. 1–11*

Sonata in D Major

Wolfgang Amadeus Mozart (1756–1791)
K. 311

(a) A dispute exists over the LH part that opens m. 1. The autograph seems to show the D major octave filled in with F-sharp
and A. The notation is small, however, and the two inner notes have been deemed by some as merely a thickening of the
stem between the two notes of the octave, especially in light of m. 99 where the LH is clearly only the octave. The first
edition shows the octave with only the A between the outer notes. Editions vary and may show any one of the three versions.

(b) The grace notes should be played as 16th notes, resulting in groups of four equal 16th notes.
See also mm. 3, 4, 6, 13, 14, 35, 61, 65, 75, 76, 94, 98, 99, 101, 102, 104, 107, and 108.

(c) [musical notation] or [musical notation]   The grace note on the downbeat is written as ♪ in the autograph. Performers are equally
divided as to the two realizations shown. *See also* m. 102.

(d) [musical notation]   *See also* m. 9.

(e) Play the grace notes in mm. 16 and 78 rapidly *before the beat.*

(f) *See also* m. 81.

(g) *See also* mm. 22, 83, and 84.

(h) or

(i) The autograph shows staccato marks on the eighth notes in mm. 87–90 but not in mm. 24–27.

(j) *See also* mm. 33, 59, 63, 92, and 96.

(k) or

See also mm. 35, 61, 65, 94, and 98.

① The first edition shows  .

174

Andante con espressione

(a) The grace notes in mm. 1, 5, 25, 27, 39, 61, 63, 76, and 79 are written as ♪ in the autograph, and the tradition of playing them *before the beat* is well established. The written-out variation in mm. 43 and 75 suggests the possibility of improvising other ornaments in the context of this theme.

(b) The autograph shows the four 16th notes in the second half of mm. 7 and 45 under one slur, while the first edition shows

(c) [music] or [music] *See also* mm. 33–35, 46, 69–71, and 82.

(d) Although the autograph shows little distinction between the notation of the grace notes noted in footnote (a) and those in mm. 9, 11, 13, 47, 49, 83, 85, 87, and 89–91, the second group has a strong performance tradition of being played as 16th notes, resulting in groups of four equal 16th notes.

(e) [music] or [music]

(f) [music] *See also* mm. 17, 52, and 53.

(g) The grace note in m. 19 should be played as a 32nd note, resulting in a group of four equal 32nd notes: [music] *See also* mm. 31, 35, 55, 67, 71, 73, and 78.

(h) Play the two grace notes rapidly *on the beat*: [music] . *See also* m. 56.

(i) Play the three grace notes as a rapid triplet *on the beat*: . *See also* m. 58.

(j) *See also* mm. 63 and 64.

The after-notes are optional. They seem graceful in m. 28 but awkward in m. 64.

(k) *See also* m. 73.

(l) Similarly, in m. 43: . *See also* m. 75.

 The grace note at the beginning of m. 47 should be played as a 16th note *on the beat*.
See also mm. 49, 85, and 87.

ⓝ ♦ or ♦ *See also* m. 84.

ⓞ The LH pattern shown in m. 55 follows the autograph. Some editors point out that it is not an exact transposition of the pattern in m. 19.

Rondeau
Allegro

(a)   The grace notes in this movement are shown as ♪ in the autograph. Those that attend eighth notes, quarter notes, and dotted quarter notes are played rapidly *before the beat*. (*See* mm. 1–4 and similar passages.) Grace notes that attend ♩♫♫ are played as a 16th note *on the beat*, resulting in groups of equal 16th notes.

(b)   Execute the figure in mm. 21 and 23 as a rapid six-note ornament, feeling the impulse of the first note (which is tied) on beat 3. *See also* mm. 107, 109, 261, and 263.

Playing the three grace notes in m. 27 rapidly as triplets on beats 1 and 4 is pianistic and preserves the rhythmic vitality of the phrase. *See also* mm. 31, 190, and 194.

See also mm. 78, 241, and 243.

ⓔ *See also* mm. 120–122, 127–130, 147, and 153.

ⓕ or *See also* m. 124.

(g) The autograph shows a different configuration of the similar ornament noted earlier. (*See* footnote (b).)
It has suggested to some performers that these later configurations represent a variation
of the ornament and that the three grace notes should be played as a rapid triplet before beat 3:

See also mm. 161, 163, 165, and 167.

(h) The trill in this improvisatory cadenza invites personal execution. It should start no quicker than the preceding 16th notes
and accelerate gradually to encompass the written-out after-notes and *Presto* chromatic scale. Because of the fermata,
the trill's duration should be longer than the six preceding 16th notes or even longer. One may even slow the trill to a halt
and play the after-notes and run as a surprise. Use imagination to create tension and to tease listeners, and apply similar freedom
to the grace notes in the following *Adagio* section.

(i) The autograph shows ♪ .

Most editions use E instead of C-sharp, since it appears in previous statements of the theme.